INSIGHT INTO

STRESS

INSIGHT INTO
STRESS

Beverley Shepherd

CWR

WAVERLEY ABBEY
INSIGHT SERIES

The Waverley Abbey Insight Series has been developed in response to the great need to help people understand and face some key issues that many of us struggle with today. CWR's ministry spans teaching, training and publishing, and this series draws on all of these areas of ministry.

Sourced from material first presented over Insight Days by CWR at their base, Waverley Abbey House, presenters and authors have worked in close co-operation to bring this series together, offering clear insight, teaching and help on a broad range of subjects and issues. Bringing biblical understanding and godly insight, these books are written both for those who help others and those who face these issues themselves.

CONTENTS

FOREWORD

There's something you need to know about Beverley Shepherd before you read this book. But I'll come to that.

Two years ago I discovered the difference between pressure and stress.

I'd been under intense pressure many times before – working in advertising on Madison Avenue, working in a theological college (yes, really), and working at the London Institute for Contemporary Christianity (quite definitely). Pressure can be unpleasant but pressure can be exhilarating, pressure can focus the mind. Pressure can be a spur to creativity, and an encouragement towards excellence.

Stress, I discovered, was something altogether different – darker, more acidic, a jangly current running through one's veins, a mind that won't shut down, emotions that are too intense, a weariness in the marrow, a loss of joy in the things that usually put a zing in the day, and the sense that it ain't going to change. And I knew from talking to others that I didn't even have it that bad.

Something I also knew was that switching to camomile tea (heaven forfend), doing deep breathing exercises and sticking a picture of a Caribbean beach on top of my computer wasn't going to make enough of a difference to deal with the real issues.

This book will help you deal with the real issues. It will help you chart the interactions between external circumstances and inner turmoil and identify the external things that might be changed and the internal attitudes that need to be addressed. Still, this is not just a book about stress management, rather it is about making the most of any stress you're facing. After all, as Beverley suggests, God might be using stress to teach us something more significant than simply how to avoid stress. As such, this is a book about liberation and spiritual flourishing, about forgiveness and repentance, about learning to hear what God is saying in the maelstrom, and about finding shalom in the maelstrom, not just an escape from it.

So here's what you need to know about Beverley Shepherd: she's not stressed.

She's been in stressful situations, certainly, and she may well be in one now, but she is one of those people who radiates a joyous peace, whose brow is not deeply furrowed by worry and whose heart always has room to listen to others. This is certainly not because she ambles through life on the income from her invested billions. On the contrary, she is a freelance management trainer – just the word 'freelance' is enough to send my stressometer soaring. But Beverley knows how to deal with stress and she knows how to help others deal with theirs. She's been doing it for years – prayerfully, thoughtfully and sensitively. She's not called 'Shepherd' for nothing.

Of course, you may be too stressed to find time to read a book on stress, if you are, this may well be the book for you. Will it be as soothing as a hot herbal bath? No, it will be more like a deep muscle massage – you might have to go through some discomfort to get the knots out but once they're out …

Shalom be with you.

Mark Greene, 2006

INTRODUCTION

Are you tired? Worn out? Burned out on religion? Come to me. Get away with me and you'll recover your life. I'll show you how to take a real rest. Walk with me and work with me – watch how I do it. Learn the unforced rhythms of grace. I won't lay anything heavy or ill-fitting on you. Keep company with me and you'll learn to live freely and lightly. (Matt. 11:28–30, *The Message*)

In a world where stress has infected both the Church and secular society, is it really possible to live 'freely and lightly'? Recent newspaper articles suggest not: 'Excessive stress at work is causing an epidemic of depression and anxiety, costing the British economy about £100bn a year in lost output' (*The Guardian*, 16 May 2005). 'Last year, more than 13 million working days were lost to stress-related illnesses in the workplace' (*The Money Programme*, 2005).

Far from offering solutions, the Church and its ministers are also feeling the effects of stress: *Evangelicals Now* (6 July 2005) conducted a survey of 300 pastors from major Protestant Christian denominations and concluded: 'Stress appears to be the greatest problem for the pastors in the UK.' Their statistics reveal that 47 per cent of pastors say that they feel stressed often or always.

The problem is not limited to the pulpit – it is evidenced in the pews as well:

A report in the UK has revealed that the demands placed upon us every day are stopping people from attending services. Exhaustion after a stressful day at work, as well as increasing commitments at the weekends have meant that many people and even entire families cannot make it to church. (*Christian Today*, 19 July 2005)

Given the prevalence of stress in our society, my aim in writing this book is to give both those who experience stress and those who work with or counsel the stressed, clearer insight and understanding of this subject. This book is written for people who live in the real world – a world in which we experience myriad pressures; where our loved ones endure pain and die; where we experience the 'present sufferings' and 'creation … subjected to frustration' and in 'bondage to decay' of Romans 8:18–21. We live in a world where the context for our work is cursed (Gen. 3:17–19) and so the photocopier will break down just when we need it, the train will be delayed and our toil will at times be painful. Yet surely the goal of each of us is not just the absence of stress but the embracing of a life that is lived 'freely and lightly', that moves, even dances, to the 'unforced rhythms of grace'. So, beyond helpful insights, my aim is also to challenge each one of us to confront the issues that stress presents – to allow stress to motivate us to seek God in a new way. It is as we are serious in doing business with God that real healing can occur.

Over the years I have had the privilege of presenting the CWR Insight Days on stress, running courses on Stress Management in the non-Christian business environment and presenting seminars on stress at various Christian conferences. The material in this book draws on that range of experience and I am thankful, in particular, to the delegates on my courses for the life stories they have shared and the questions and challenges they have posed which have caused me to constantly review and revise my material to ensure its relevance and effectiveness.

CHAPTER 1

WHAT IS STRESS?

To effectively manage stress in ourselves or others we have to first understand what it is. The Health & Safety Executive's definition is one of the clearest and most helpful – stress is:

> the adverse reaction people have to excessive pressure or other types of demand placed upon them.[1]

This definition allows us to address this subject by asking such questions as:

- What are the pressures a person experiences?
- What determines a person's individual reaction?
- How is this reaction to be observed and monitored?
- At what point is the reaction deemed to be 'adverse'?

Pressure of itself is not a bad thing – most of us respond positively to pressure by mobilising our energy and efficiency, focusing our thoughts and getting on with it. Some would say that they thrive on pressure and would find the absence of it to be stressful! One helpful way of understanding the impact of pressure is the pressure/performance curve, outlining a range of reactions as pressure increases.[2]

The pressure/performance stages

Adapted from Managing Workplace Stress by Stephen Williams and Lesley Cooper

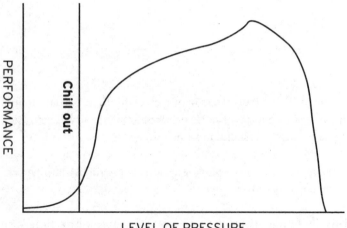

Chill out

At low levels of pressure, there is often low performance, ie on those days when nothing much needs doing, nothing much gets done! There is nothing wrong with this, we all need chill out days in which to recharge our batteries, change down a few gears and watch the sun set.

Work out

In the 'work out' zone every increase in pressure brings a corresponding upturn in performance. As the pressure increases we think more rapidly, move faster and make decisions more quickly. The key aspect of this zone is that it is sustainable – we can do it again tomorrow and the next day and the next. We are well within our ability to cope and can often get a great deal of satisfaction from how much we feel we are achieving as we move up the curve.

Stretch

In the 'stretch' zone the performance curve is still going up. Now the adrenalin is flowing, we are pulling out all the stops, and we are delivering! Yet we are also aware that we are emptying the cupboard – depleting our reserves. Underneath all the activity is the awareness that we cannot carry on at this pace – we need an end point, a deadline, a stop date – after which time we know we will be able to relax. Having run courses in several schools, teachers often identify 'stretch' with the last two weeks before the end of term – that final day of school is highlighted in their calendar and they are hanging on in there with the thought 'if I can just make it through to term end, then I can collapse.' If our 'end point' gets postponed or cancelled, or the pressures continue to mount, then we may find ourselves in strain.

Strain

In the 'strain' zone we have gone past the maximum effective pressure point and are heading down the slippery slope. This is the area that corresponds with the HSE definition of stress, ie an adverse reaction to pressure. Now things are starting to go wrong – mistakes at work, failure to communicate, increased likelihood of illness … we feel unable to cope, with life getting out of control. Should the pressures continue then we are at risk of damaging ourselves physically, emotionally and in our relationships.

Burnout

People experiencing 'burnout' often feel angry, helpless, trapped and totally depleted. This experience is more intense than what is ordinarily called stress. Usually people have been under considerable pressure for a prolonged period and this may have been aggravated by personal conflicts and unattainable goals. 'The major defining characteristic of burnout is that people can't or won't do again what they have been doing.'[3] Cynicism and negativity often accompany the burnout experience.

Christina Maslach, a researcher on the subject at the University of California at Berkeley, says that burnout 'refers to a syndrome of emotional exhaustion and cynicism that frequently occurs among people who do "people work" – who spend considerable time in close encounters'.[4]

RECOGNISING THE SIGNS

It is important to identify where we are on the pressure/performance curve because by the time we have reached the higher end of stretch and are moving into strain we have very little energy for taking remedial action. How then can we recognise which area of the curve we currently inhabit? The symptoms of stress are wide ranging and cover our physiology, behaviour, intellect, emotions and spiritual life. No two people have the same symptoms and the effects may vary considerably

– for instance, a common symptom is that eating patterns are affected, with one person eating more sugary foods and gaining weight whereas another may not be bothered with food and lose weight as a result.

It should also be noted that the symptoms listed below may have causes other than stress. The key thing is to learn to monitor your own stress reactions and develop a personal 'early warning system'.

Physical

Our bodies are designed to physically react to a threat through the 'Fight or Flight' response. When posed with a physical threat our bodies prepare to either run away or to fight. This preparation involves blood being diverted away from certain internal organs – particularly the digestive system – to muscle groups around the arms and legs. This requires our heart rate to increase, blood pressure to go up and our ability to digest food to deteriorate. A fighting stance is adopted – the muscles around the shoulders and neck tense, the jaw locks and the eyes narrow. These reactions are appropriate and can be a life saver if physical action is then required. However, when we develop these responses to the size of our email in-tray; the irritations of particular colleagues or family members, traffic congestion, the level of our bank balance then we are likely to develop certain physical symptoms over time: muscular tension, aches and pains, loss of appetite or over indulgence in sugar, alcohol or nicotine, high blood pressure, headaches and always feeling tired. Our immune system becomes depleted and we are vulnerable to every cough, cold or flu bug that is doing the rounds.

Emotional

It is often those who are closest to us at work or at home that are most aware of the changes in our emotional responses. As one woman told me, 'I always know how stressed I am – my teenagers tell me!' These emotional reactions include irritability, anger, depression, impatience, loss of confidence and worrying excessively.

Social

Some people withdraw as a result of stress – the answerphone goes on, the office door closes, and social chat feels like a waste of time. 'Stay away world, you've had all you are going to get of me!' is the message they give out. Others however become frenetic, filling every moment with activity, in an effort not to have to think.

Intellectual

Just when we need to be thinking clearly and making our best decisions, the ability to do so vanishes. We find it difficult to concentrate, lack judgment and reason, and decisions seem impossibly complicated.

Spiritual

Spiritual responses vary but can include the inability to pray, loss of purpose or hope, doubting God's goodness, blaming God for allowing things to turn out this way, withdrawal from fellowship with other Christians, and feeling victimised and helpless. Others allow the pressure of their situation to drive them closer to God.

Team

In any team or group situation the effects of individual stress show themselves in a variety of ways: sickness absence; staff turnover leading to skill lost and additional recruitment costs; reduced service levels as motivation deteriorates; an increase in the number of accidents; absenteeism; presenteeism (where people show up for work but are incapable of producing good work); poor decision making; loss of creativity and innovation; erosion of employee goodwill; and withdrawal of discretionary effort.

Understanding what stress is and how to recognise it are important but form part of a journey – a journey that will lead us to identify the pressures that brought us to this point and to explore God's way forward into healing.

CHAPTER 2

THE WARNING LIGHT

Stress is a reaction – specifically a reaction to pressure. Although this reaction may have many negative symptoms physically, emotionally, intellectually etc as we saw in the last chapter, stress of itself is not the problem. It is like a warning light on the dashboard of a car – it alerts us to the fact that something else is wrong. The answer is not to disconnect the red light but to address the underlying problem. Too often organisations and churches deal with stress in their employees by, metaphorically, taking the car off the road for several weeks or months – the warning light goes out because the engine has been switched off, yet as soon as the car is back on the road it can only drive very slowly or the red light will reappear. Rarely is time spent dealing with the underlying issues.

To deal effectively with the root problem we need a working

model of the stress mechanism, the different pressures a person experiences, and the effect of varying 'stress-relieving' interventions. The diagram on the opposite page is one such model.

THE METAL SPRING

Picture yourself as a metal spring. You are designed to carry weight, to extend as you do so, and then to go back into shape when the weights are removed. Life is a sequence of extension – relax – extension – relax, and so on. The problems arise in three main ways:

- The spring becomes weak
- The weights are too heavy or stay on the spring too long
- Support or help in carrying the load is non-existent or removed

The weights represent the different pressures we each experience. I have grouped these into five main categories:

Change: This includes 'life events' such as birth, marriage, death, moving house, changing job, family illness etc.

The demands and expectations of others: workload, deadlines, our roles at church, family expectations and the never-ending 'To Do' list all come under this area.

Self-expectation: Often self-expectation is one of the primary factors in stress because it is not just another weight on the spring – it is a multiplier. It multiplies the effects of the two preceding weights.

Understanding Stress

**CHANGE AND
UNCERTAINTY**
(Life events)

**DEMANDS AND
EXPECTATIONS
OF OTHERS**

SELF-EXPECTATION
(Drivenness)

LACK OF PURPOSE
(Demotivation and
resentment)

ATTACK
(Personal, physical
and spiritual)

Lack of purpose/demotivation/resentment: again have a multiply-ing effect. Any task, however little time it takes, that we resent having to do, becomes a significant weight on our spring.

Personal, physical and spiritual attack: In Ephesians we are told that 'our struggle is not against flesh and blood, but against the rulers, against the authorities, against the powers of this dark world and against the spiritual forces of evil in the heavenly realms' (Eph. 6:12).

In each of the next five chapters we will examine these pressures in more detail, look at a biblical case study for each, and seek effective strategies that can be applied to our individual situations. Subsequent chapters will address 'strengthening the spring' and gaining support.

CASE STUDY: ELIJAH

> Elijah was afraid and ran for his life. ... He came to a broom tree, sat down under it and prayed that he might die. 'I have had enough, LORD,' he said. 'Take my life; I am no better that my ancestors.' (1 Kings 19:3–4)

The Elijah of Kings 19 seems a very different person from the prophet on Mount Carmel of the previous chapter. We see him running for his life, tired, worn out, depressed and wanting to end it all. Unlike previous journeys where he has been clearly directed by God to go to Kerith, then Zarephath and finally to present himself to Ahab, here the motivation for his journey is fear. Perversely the very reason he is on the run is because Jezebel

24

has threatened to kill him and then he prays to God that he might die! What has brought him to this point?

We learn that he is emotionally, spiritually and physically worn out, for the journey is too much for him, yet the day before he was running faster than Ahab's chariot. He has been falsely accused by Ahab, the very person who has led Israel into idolatry and Baal worship, of being the 'troubler of Israel' (1 Kings 18:17). He has been engaged in a spiritual battle for three and a half years on behalf of his nation, much of this hidden from public gaze. He has confronted and defeated the prophets of Baal and yet this seems to have produced no change of heart in Ahab or Jezebel. Without godly leadership he knows that the people will soon return to their old ways, despite their declaration that they will follow God. He has lost his vision and motivation, feeling alone and victimised, as he declares to God: 'I have been very zealous for the LORD God Almighty. The Israelites have rejected your covenant, broken down your altars, and put your prophets to death with the sword. I am the only one left, and now they are trying to kill me too' (1 Kings 19:10). With a viewpoint distorted by tiredness, loneliness and disappointment ('I am no better than my ancestors', v.4) it is little wonder that he doesn't feel there is much point in going on.

What is the response of God to this prophet who seems to have lost the plot and run away from the very people to whom God has called him to minister? Is it to rebuke him? No, it is here in the wilderness, rather than on the top of Mount Carmel, that God chooses to give His worn-out servant proof of His love and care. God, who is Lord of our bodies, provides for his rest and refreshment by sending an angel to minister to him. Yet again Elijah experiences the personal provision of God. Before, he had received food via the ravens and the widow, now it is baked for him by an angel. God deals gently and lovingly with His worn-out servant, listening as Elijah pours out his heart – twice!

For the first time, though, Elijah's prayer is not answered. He asks that he may die. In fact it is never answered! Elijah, instead of dying, ascends to heaven in a whirlwind (2 Kings 2:11). Why is it now, when Elijah is at his lowest point, that his prayer is rejected? I believe it is because this is the first time that Elijah has not prayed as a servant, seeking to carry out God's will. On Mount Carmel his prayer was: 'O LORD, God of Abraham, Isaac and Israel, let it be known today that you are God in Israel and that I am your servant and have done all these things at your command' (1 Kings 18:36). Here in the wilderness he presents his situation to God: 'I have had enough,' but then seeks to instruct God as to the solution: 'Take my life.' God will never answer prayer where we seek to dictate to Him how He is to act. A more appropriate prayer for Elijah's situation might have been that of Jehoshaphat in 2 Chronicles 20:12: '... we have no power to face this vast army that is attacking us. We do not know what to do, but our eyes are upon you.'

In journeying to Horeb, Elijah is allowing his distress to drive him to seek God. It may seem strange that this man who has known God's amazing provision, has on several occasions had very clear direction, has seen extraordinary answers to prayer with the dead being raised and fire falling from heaven, now feels the need to seek God in a new way.

Horeb, the mount of God, was certainly a remarkable place for Elijah to make for, for there was no spot on earth where the presence of God was so signally manifested as there, at least in Old Testament times.

> It was there that Jehovah had appeared unto Moses at the burning
> bush, Ex. 3:1–4. It was there that the Law had been given to Israel,
> Deut. 4:15, under such awe-inspiring phenomena. It was there that
> Moses had communed with Him for forty days and nights.[1]

And it is here at Horeb that God reveals Himself and His character to Elijah.

When God had given the Law to Moses at Horeb it was accompanied by thunder, lightning, smoke and an earthquake (Exod. 19:16–19). Now, in front of Elijah the same manifestations appear: 'Then a great and powerful wind tore the mountains apart and shattered the rocks before the Lord, but the Lord was not in the wind. After the wind there was an earthquake, but the Lord was not in the earthquake. After the earthquake came a fire, but the Lord was not in the fire' (1 Kings 19:11–12). Why was the Lord not in the wind, earthquake or fire? Because the Lord is not now meeting with Elijah as the God of the Law but as the God of Grace! God lovingly speaks to Elijah in a still (calm) small voice, re-commissioning him and giving him a task to accomplish. To this prophet who has lost hope He gives His heavenly perspective and assurance of the ultimate victory of God's cause. To this man who had begun to think that he was God's only instrument in saving Israel, God gently points out that He has other instruments and that saving Israel is His responsibility and not Elijah's! And to the prophet who feels very alone, God promises a companion and help-mate – Elisha.

PERSONAL APPLICATION

What might the example of Elijah be saying to God's servants today who 'have had enough'?

- Allow the Lord to restore you physically through sleep and a healthy diet.
- Receive those that God sends to minister to you – even though they are not the ones you had expected to be your support! God's angels are often disguised in human form.
- Present your situation to the Lord in prayer but do not dictate the solution.
- Know that God wants to meet with you as the God of Grace.
- Allow yourself to become still inside so that you can hear the gentle whisper of God – it may take forty days!
- Ask for God's perspective on your situation – ours is often distorted through weariness, loneliness and fear.
- Allow the pressures you are experiencing to drive you to seek God in new ways.

CHAPTER 3

CHANGE

The first of the five 'weights' on the spring, or areas of pressure, is change. Most of us welcome some degree of change, so why then is it viewed as a key stressor? The answer lies in the effect change has on us, particularly when we have not chosen the change and are not in control of the outcomes. Change moves us out of our comfort zone: we can no longer operate on automatic pilot but have to 'engage brain', assess options or just wait to be told what others have decided for us. Even in a change we may have chosen, such has moving house, there are a number of variables over which we have no control – for example the other people in the 'chain', the time taken to do surveys and land searches, the new neighbours.

In a famous study in 1967, Dr Thomas H. Holmes and Dr Richard H. Rahe were among the first to identify a correlation between the amount of change a person went through in a given period and stress (indicated by the likelihood of them becoming ill). They developed the Social Readjustment Rating Scale, which identifies and ranks eighty-seven key stressful life-change events in six major aspects of life adjustment: health, work, family, personal, social and financial. The points total, gained by identifying the number of life events a person had experienced in a twelve-month period, was then used to predict the likelihood that a person would experience a stress-related illness or accident within the next two years. At the top of their scale were events such as the death of your spouse (100 points) and divorce (75). Retirement at 45 was only slightly lower than redundancy at 47, whereas marriage scored 50 and Christmas, 12! Whatever we may think of the relative values assigned to the different life events, their conclusions that change causes pressure and leads to stress-related illness are not in dispute.

Our reaction to any life event is determined by our perception of that event. For instance, put three people in a room with a large hairy non-poisonous spider and one may run out of the door in panic whilst another examines the spider, intrigued. The third shows not the slightest interest. Perception of any particular change is governed by a range of factors including upbringing, culture, age, experience, support, financial security and beliefs. In working with people facing redundancy, reactions can range from 'Great, I'm out of here', through 'I really didn't need this right now' and 'How am I going to pay the mortgage?' to 'Where will I get another job?' or 'How can they do this to me?'

Take a moment to identify the amount of change you have experienced in the last twelve months:

Change

On the grid below, note any significant changes you have experienced in the last 12 months, irrespective of whether you view those changes to be positive or negative.

Work:

Home and Family:

Friends and Social:

Self (including health & finances):

THE GRIEF CYCLE

Elizabeth Kübler-Ross, a doctor in Switzerland, wrote a book called *On Death and Dying* which included a cycle of emotional states that is often referred to as the Grief Cycle.[1] In the ensuing years, it was noticed that this emotional cycle was not exclusive to the terminally ill, but also applied to other people who were affected by bad news, such as losing their jobs or otherwise being negatively affected by change. The important factor is not that the change was good or bad, but that they *perceived* it as a significantly negative event.

The Grief Cycle indicates the roller-coaster ride of activity and passivity as the person wriggles and turns in his or her desperate efforts to avoid the change. The cycle assumes an initial position of stability before the change happens.

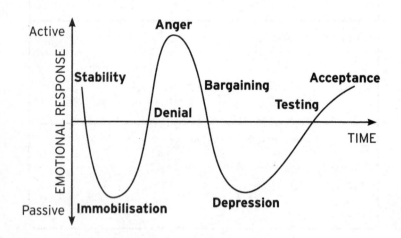

- Shock stage: Initial paralysis at hearing the bad news.
- Denial stage: Trying to avoid the inevitable.
- Anger stage: Frustrated outpouring of bottled-up emotion.
- Bargaining stage: Seeking in vain for a way out.
- Depression stage: Final realisation of the inevitable.
- Testing stage: Seeking realistic solutions.
- Acceptance stage: Finally finding the way forward.

Acceptance and assimilation of the change are not always guaranteed, as people can get 'stuck' at various stages of the curve – particularly in anger or depression.

As Christians, how are we to move through the changes in our lives to ensure acceptance and not depression? Our beliefs are central to this process. They are like anchors in a storm. Three key anchors we have are:

- God is in control
- God is good
- Nothing can happen to me that God has not permitted

When any one of these is cut loose we become vulnerable to the full turbulence of the storm. Yet it is often in tragic circumstances that these very beliefs are thrown into question and we doubt either God's goodness, omnipotence or both. In Jane Grayshon's book *Treasures of Darkness* the story is told of a young mother, Sarah, who watched her young son Robert die. Sarah describes one traumatic night as follows:

> All of one night beside Robert's cot I remember looking helplessly on, weeping and sobbing. I felt as if I'd reached rock bottom by then.

I cried out, 'Lord, please don't ask me to go through with Robert dying!' And there was no response; only the constant repetition of the question, 'Do you believe in the goodness of God?' Somewhere – somewhere – among all my fear, I was aware of a flicker of hope. I knew it had to be a lie to imagine that God would impose dreadful things on me, disregarding me. It seemed as if He was, but deep down I knew it wasn't true. To acknowledge the lie was like the glimmering dawn light. I had to concede that His purposes are for good and not for evil … The only peaceful course for me was to trust in God's goodness.[2]

Joni Eareckson Tada was a fit and healthy young woman when a diving accident severed her spinal column and left her paralysed. She wrestled with the sovereignty of God – if He was truly sovereign then He could have saved her from this fate.

The idea that God could have prevented my accident but didn't, hurt me deeply. The idea that He planned it appalled me. That He planned it for my good and His glory horrified me. Was He using some other dictionary than the human race uses?

Eventually the light and dazzling truth of God's sovereignty began to dawn. She came to understand that 'God screens the trials that come to each of us – allowing only those that accomplish His good plan because He takes no joy in human agony. Nothing happens by accident … not even tragedy … not even sins committed against us. God is in control, not in a general way, but in a very specific way.' The result of this truth brought a new attitude to her accident:

I cannot begin to express the relief and release I felt as I plunged deeper into this marvellous truth that my diving accident was really no accident at all. Finally … I yielded. I submitted. I exhaled a long, slow, satisfied breath and relaxed into the sovereign arms of God. If He loved me enough to die for me, then trusting Him with quadriplegia should be a cinch.[3]

Few of us have had to test the doctrines of God's goodness and sovereignty in the ways that Sarah and Joni have, yet they apply equally to all the circumstances of our lives and can bring the same peace. When we lay down our perceived right to know why things happen and stop demanding that God make Himself accountable to us, we can begin to ask Him the more important question: 'Lord, how would you have me respond to this situation?'

God has placed us in a family – the Church. We are not expected to face the storms of life alone. At each stage of the Grief Cycle, help and support are needed to move us through to the next stage. Much of this can be very practical – I am grateful to the friend who came with me to register my father's death, sat and chatted with me during the half-hour wait and then took me for a coffee. In designing the order of service for his funeral, another friend spent time searching through her considerable clip-art collection to find a picture of a thistle to represent Dad's Scottish origins. Cards and flowers expressing love, care and prayer support are invaluable at such times. Our Bible reading can also help us get in touch with and express our emotions – particularly certain of the Psalms and Lamentations.

CASE STUDY: ELIMELECH AND NAOMI

> In the days when the judges ruled, there was a famine in the land, and a man from Bethlehem in Judah, together with his wife and two sons, went to live for a while in the country of Moab. The man's name was Elimelech, his wife's name Naomi, and the names of his two sons were Mahlon and Kilion. They were Ephrathites from Bethlehem, Judah. And they went to Moab and lived there. Now Elimelech, Naomi's husband, died, and she was left with her two sons. They married Moabite women, one named Orpah and the other Ruth. After they had lived there about ten years, both Mahlon and Kilion also died, and Naomi was left without her two sons and her husband.
> (Ruth 1:1–5)

The book of Ruth, sandwiched between the Old Testament books of Judges and 1 Samuel, is carefully crafted by its unknown author – every word is there for a reason.

Throughout the book of Judges there are two refrains: the first is Israel again 'did evil in the eyes of the LORD' (Judg. 3:7,12; 4:1; 6:1; 10:6; 13:1). Each time this refrain introduces another cycle of rebellion, oppression, distress and deliverance through the Lord raising up a judge. The second refrain is 'In those days Israel had no king; everyone did as he saw fit' (Judg. 17:6; 21:25).

The story of the book of Ruth takes place in Bethlehem and in Moab and a strange contrast is drawn between them by the author. Bethlehem (meaning House of Bread, or the place of God's provision) is experiencing a famine as a result of God's judgment. Moab (meaning 'nothingness'), however, is experiencing a time of plenty. Elimelech, Naomi and their two sons find food and a welcome in Moab – they become integrated in Moabite society, intermarrying with the local girls, and staying much longer than the 'for a while' of verse 1 suggests. Yet Moab is dubious territory for the people of God with no Moabite being allowed to enter the assembly of the Lord (Deut. 23:3–6). The Moabites worshipped Chemosh – a god who required child sacrifice.

Elimelech

The author zeroes in on one family – Mum, Dad and two boys. The man is Elimelech meaning 'My God is King'. This man's very name declared the truth that Israel did have a king, despite the refrain of Judges, and that that king was God. Elimelech is living in an age (not unlike our own) where the kingship of God has been rejected (1 Sam. 8:6–7). Elimelech, responsible for the provision and welfare of his family, is faced with changing economic circumstances as a result of the famine. The author subtly poses the questions: 'Will this man live up to his name, or will he go with the prevailing culture and do what he sees fit in his own eyes?', 'Will he walk by faith or by sight?', and 'Will he trust God to save him and his family, or will he be self-reliant?'

Unfortunately Ruth 1:1 leads us to the conclusion that this man, despite his name, does not follow the advice of Proverbs 3:5 to 'Trust in the LORD with all your heart and lean not on your own understanding'. Instead he takes matters into his own hands, ignores the warnings against Moab in Deuteronomy, and moves his family to Moab. The continuing story supports this conclusion as he and his sons die – presumably the fate they were hoping to escape in Bethlehem. To further emphasise this, the 'whole town' is stirred and recognises Naomi when she eventually returns to Bethlehem with Ruth (1:19) so few, if any, had died. There may not have been plenty in the place of God's provision – but there was enough!

Naomi

Naomi's experience could well cause us to conclude that life is unfair – why should Naomi be called upon to suffer so much? First she is uprooted from her home and friends to go and live in Moab, an alien culture where Chemosh, not Yahweh, is worshipped. Then her husband dies, and within the next few years she loses both her sons. For a woman in that society, the loss of your men-folk meant not only the deep pain of bereavement, but also the loss of your status, your means of provision and your role – you were thrown onto the charity of strangers. She had gone to Moab full, but is now empty (1:21). No wonder she declares in 1:13 'the LORD's hand has gone out against me!' and 'the Almighty has made my life very bitter' (1:20). Yet here are the very seeds of hope – ultimately these are statements of God's sovereignty. God is both Lord and Almighty. It is when she returns to Bethlehem, the place of God's provision, that family, security and purpose are restored to her.

PERSONAL APPLICATION

- It is all too easy to point the finger of criticism at Elimelech and fail to realise that that leaves three fingers pointing back at us! In these first two verses of the book of Ruth we are faced with the same questions as Elimelech: 'Will we live up to our name of "Christians" – meaning "little Christs", or will we go with the prevailing culture and do what seems fit in our own eyes?', 'Will we trust God to save us and our family, or will we be self-reliant?', and 'Will we walk by faith or by sight?' When faced with a seeming deficiency in God's provision and in the context of a godless society, is our answer any different from that of Elimelech – to place our trust somewhere other than in God?

- Although we may be battered by circumstances and suffer great loss, God is still in control – there is someone to whom we can address our anguished questions: 'Why?', 'How long?', 'Do you care?', 'Have you forgotten to be merciful?' God answers our questions, not with words, but with a cross. Through the cross of Christ, God declares: 'I love you deeply, My mercy is unfailing – I know and share your pain and anguish.' The Christian life is not trouble-free – we experience the same hardships as non-believers, and it is right that we should grieve. Yet we do so in the knowledge of His sovereignty and in the security of His mercy. More than this, we know that God shares in our suffering and comforts us in our loss.

CHAPTER 4

THE DEMANDS AND EXPECTATIONS OF OTHERS

The demands and expectations of others can seem overwhelming at times. We run around in ever-decreasing circles trying to complete a 'To Do' list that seems to grow at a faster rate than we can cross items off. Our lives are filled to overflowing and to even create the space with which to examine the problem can seem impossible. All of this has conspired to convince us of the fundamental lie of time management – that there isn't enough time! Yes, most of us hold this deep-seated belief that we don't have sufficient time. All humanity has not succumbed equally, of course. Sociologists in several countries have found that increasing wealth and increasing education bring a sense of tension about time. So we believe that we possess too little of it: that is the myth we now live by. Delegates on Time Management courses give a standard reply to the question 'How many more hours a day would you need to make your life work?' – their answer: two–three hours.

Time is now a negative status symbol – the more time you have on your hands, the less important you must be. In his article 'It Boosts the Credibility', writer Michael Lewis points out that the transformation of time into a negative status has odd social consequences:

> It boosts the credibility of things that happen quickly. It also infuses with wonderful new prestige any new time saving device. After all, who most needs such a device? People who have no time! And who has the least time? The best people![1]

If we are to challenge and dethrone the belief that there isn't enough time we have to take a good look at the character of God the Creator. God is a God of abundance – we see it all around us. Millions of seeds, but only a few may be germinated. Millions of stars, but only one may be inhabited. Five thousand fed, and twelve baskets left over. Is it possible that this abundantly generous God should be stingy in one area of His creation – time? That He should have deliberately withheld those much needed extra two hours a day? That He should have 'prepared in advance', good works for us to do (Eph: 2:10) and yet not given us enough time to do them? No! God has given us more than enough time – even time to waste! Yet how do we not only believe it but start to live it?

SPIRITUAL 'TIME MANAGEMENT' PRINCIPLES

Although I have called these 'Time Management' principles, the reality is that we cannot manage time – it is a given: it will continue at 60 seconds per minute, 60 minutes per hour, 168 hours per week etc. until God calls it to an end, and there is not a thing you or I can do about it! All time management is really self-management and as such requires personal disciplines and godly wisdom. First it can be helpful to review our different roles, responsibilities and the expectations that go with them, using the table on the next page. (Please adapt it to reflect your life.)

In the table enter the demands and expectations you experience in the different roles in your life. Then enter the things you feel it is important to contribute to this role or relationship. Prayerfully consider any mismatches between the two columns. How do you feel about the page as a whole – does it seem about right or does it leave you feeling overwhelmed?

In any areas where the expectations are unclear, it is important that we clarify these with the people involved. Just because an expectation is there, does not mean that it is right for us to fulfil it (unless we have already contracted to do so). Every expectation has to be prayerfully considered and God's wisdom sought as to a godly response. That godly response may be 'No'. To do this we first have to stop.

Demands and expectations of:	The things that are important for me to contribute to this role/ relationship
My spouse:	
My family:	
My friends	
My employer/manager:	
My colleagues:	
My customers/clients:	
My church:	
Other:	

1) STOPPING

Why don't we stop? We have convinced ourselves that stopping is a luxury we cannot afford. Increasingly this world's music encourages us to maximise the use of every moment, multi-task at every opportunity – make that call on your mobile while driving, read that article while eating and give time to your spouse while watching TV. Our lives have stopped making sense. Like a long paragraph with all the punctuation and spaces between words taken out, our lives fail to convey any meaning.

> We humans have chosen speed and we thrive on it – more than we generally admit. Our ability to work fast and play fast gives us power. It thrills us. If we have learned the name of just one hormone, it is adrenaline. 'Time is a gentle deity,' said Sophocles. Perhaps it was, for him. Today it cracks the whip.[2]

Stopping is a lost skill – when we do stop we fail to appreciate the moment. At red traffic lights we anxiously tap our hand on the wheel waiting for them to go green. In a supermarket queue we bemoan the delays caused by the person in front.

> Inherent in stopping is the idea of creating enough space in your life, whether for thirty seconds or forty days, to make sure that you have first things first, that you are not so distracted that you lose the moments of meaning in life, whatever else you may be in the process of gaining.[3]

Stopping for a few moments, an afternoon, a weekend is a chance for us to regain those parts of our very self that we have lost the use of – our innocence, our spontaneity, our playfulness and our laughter. Stop! and reclaim them. Learn how to laugh again and take time to put first things first.

2) CLEARING AWAY THE RUBBLE

I am struck that when Nehemiah and the Israelites sought to rebuild the walls around Jerusalem they had first to remove the rubble: 'The strength of the labourers is giving out, and there is so much rubble that we cannot rebuild the wall' (Neh. 4:10). Often, before we can rebuild a godly use of time in our lives we have to remove the rubble of habitual time-wasting. By reviewing our use of time over a two-week period, noting how every quarter of an hour is spent, we can begin to pick out patterns of time-wasting. I am definitely not suggesting that every minute needs to be filled with activity, but when the average time spent in front of the TV per person is 21 hours a week in the UK we may need to ask ourselves some searching questions. Each of us has 168 hours in a week. By the time we have deducted at least 48 for sleep, 40 for work, and 20 for washing/dressing/eating and travel to/from work that leaves us with 60 hours of discretionary time per week at the very most. Any activity that takes six hours a week is something we are devoting 10 per cent of our discretionary life to! Surely that makes it worth prayerfully reviewing?

3) SOLITUDE

Solitude is one of the ancient Christian disciplines and probably the one we most need to regain in our present age. We often fail to realise how much we pick up the priorities, pace and attitudes of those around us. As Dallas Willard challengingly puts it:

> The normal course of day-to-day human interactions locks us into
> patterns of feeling, thought, and action that are geared to a world set

against God. Nothing but solitude can allow the development of a freedom from the ingrained behaviours that hinder our integration into God's order.

> It takes twenty times more the amount of amphetamine to kill individual mice than it takes to kill them in groups. Experimenters also find that a mouse given no amphetamine at all will be dead within ten minutes of being placed in the midst of a group on the drug. In groups they go off like popcorn or fireworks. Western men and women, especially, talk a great deal about being individuals but our conformity to social pattern is hardly less remarkable than that of the mice – and just as deadly!
>
> In solitude we find the psychic distance, the perspective from which we can see, in the light of eternity, the created things that trap, worry, and oppress us.[4]

It isn't always easy to find solitude and to take time, within that solitude, to hear again God's still small voice. It means carving out an afternoon, a day, a week or longer, where we place ourselves outside the reach of the normal interruptions, telephone calls and activities and allow our minds, hearts and spirits to become still.

4) SEASONS

> There is a time for everything, and a season for every activity under heaven: a time to be born and a time to die. ... What does the worker gain from his toil? I have seen the burden God has laid on men. He has made everything beautiful in its time. He has also set eternity in the hearts of men; yet they cannot fathom what God has done from beginning to end. (Eccl. 3:1–2,9–11)

God has given us seasons – times of hectic activity and times of rest, yet we often live as if there were only one season – harvest. We attempt to reap what we have not sown and build without foundations. Instead of working from a place of rest, we collapse exhausted from our work. Looking at my garden, there seem to be four main seasons – rest, growth, fruit-bearing/harvest and pruning. It's important to know which season we are in and to allow those around us to be in a different season.

Problems come when we get the season wrong, or feel criticised by others. It seems to me that this happened to Martha. It's not wrong to be busy – many of our church activities would close if it were not for the faithful work of the Marthas. Yet this was the season before Christ's death – the last opportunity to sit at His feet and learn from Him, the last opportunity to be intimate with Him – and Mary had known and sat at His feet. Martha, wrongly judging the season, perhaps through habitual patterns of busyness, had found herself worried and upset about many things, critical of Mary and rebuked by Jesus.

Getting the season wrong for King David led to adultery and murder:

> In the spring, at the time when kings go off to war, David sent Joab out with the king's men ... but David remained in Jerusalem. One evening David got up from his bed and walked around on the roof of the palace. From the roof he saw a woman bathing.' (2 Sam. 11:1–2).

The rest, as they say, is history![5]

5) WORKING FROM REST

In the Old Testament we learn that God rested from His work

on the seventh day. In the New Testament our Sabbath changed to the first day of the week. We now start our week with rest! The Sabbath was designed by God to be the time when we stop and regain His perspective on who He is; our redemption and who He created us to be; and what it means to be channels of His blessing into this fallen world. What better way to start the week! In practice, I have also found it to be the time when I have the opportunity to lay the forthcoming week before God and seek His wisdom and guidance – only then can I say 'Yes' without reservation and 'No' without guilt. 'In repentance and rest is your salvation, in quietness and trust is your strength …' (Isa. 30:15)

CASE STUDY: JESUS

> Are you tired? Worn out? Burned out on religion? Come to me. Get away with me and you'll recover your life. I'll show you how to take a real rest. Walk with me and work with me – watch how I do it. Learn the unforced rhythms of grace. I won't lay anything heavy or ill-fitting on you. Keep company with me and you'll learn to live freely and lightly. (Matt. 11:28–30, *The Message*)

'Watch how I do it,' Jesus says. The Gospels offer us a wonderful opportunity for doing just this. Two occasions in Mark's Gospel are particularly instructive.

> Very early in the morning, while it was still dark, Jesus got up, left the house and went off to a solitary place, where he prayed. Simon and his companions went to look for him, and when they found him, they exclaimed: 'Everyone is looking for you!' Jesus replied,

'Let us go somewhere else – to the nearby villages – so I can preach there also. That is why I have come.' (Mark 1:35–38)

The word had gone out – if you wanted healing or deliverance, then Jesus was your man. Just the evening before He had healed all the sick and demon-possessed people that were brought to Him. So why, in verse 38, does He ignore all those needy people who are looking for Him and go on to the nearby villages? It can only be that, through time alone with His Father, He has received a clear understanding of His purpose and the priorities that flow from that. None of us can be in two places at once and when we have understood from God what our 'Yes' should be, then we have to say 'No' to everything else.

PERSONAL APPLICATION

- Time with God is the top priority – many of us would acknowledge this, but do our diaries reflect it?
- We then get our other priorities from Him.
- Jesus came to serve, but people were not His master.
- When we receive our priorities from God we can say NO without guilt because we know what we are to say YES to.
- There is enough time to do God's will.

However…

The apostles gathered around Jesus and reported to him all they had done and taught. Then, because so many people were coming and going that they did not even have a chance to eat, he said to them, 'Come with me by yourselves to a quiet place and get some rest.' So they went away by themselves in a boat to a solitary place. But many who saw them leaving recognised them and ran on foot from all the towns and got there ahead of them. When Jesus landed and saw a large crowd, he had compassion on them, because they were like sheep without a shepherd. So he began teaching them many things. (Mark 6:30–34)

If the incident in Mark 1 left the impression that we are to be rigid in sticking to our timetable for the day, then this occasion in Mark 6 gives a helpful balance. Here we see Jesus responding with compassion to this shepherd-less crowd.

PERSONAL APPLICATION

- Jesus wants us, His disciples, to rest.
- Compassion should lead us to seek God's wisdom as to how to respond to the needs of a situation.
- It will require flexibility to respond to what God is showing you in that moment.

CHAPTER 5

SELF-EXPECTATION

Let me introduce you to Paul – Paul is an activist:

A disproportionate amount of his emotional energies are consumed struggling against the normal constraints of time. 'How can I move faster, and do more and more things in less and less time?' is the question that never ceases to torment him. Paul hurries his thinking, his speech and his movements. He also strives to hurry the thinking, speech and movements of those about him; they must communicate rapidly and relevantly if they wish to avoid creating impatience in him. Planes must arrive and depart precisely on time for Paul, cars ahead of him on the motorway must maintain a speed that he approves of, there must never be a queue of persons standing between him and a bank clerk, a restaurant table, or a rail ticket office. In fact, he is infuriated whenever people talk slowly, when planes are late, cars dawdle, and queues form.[1]

We smile, but unfortunately I do identify with Paul rather more than I generally care to admit, and so do some of you. We may not have the activist disease as badly as Paul, but we can feel tyrannised by the urgent, collapse exhausted in front of the TV with a list of chores still on our 'To Do' list; and anxiously spend time reading books on time-saving techniques and researching multi-tasking opportunities. Bestseller lists are filled with manuals with such 'optimistic' titles as *How to Have a 48 Hour Day*, or *More Time for Sex*; publishers direct parents to books of 'one-minute bedtime stories'; while lifts have non-operative 'close door' buttons to give impatient executives the illusion that they are in control!

Activism is only one form of self-expectation – others include perfectionism, people-pleasing, being the 'saviour' and striving. We will look at these in more detail later but first it is important to understand how drivenness develops.

THE ORPHAN SPIRIT

> But for those like us, our fate is to face the world as orphans, chasing through long years the shadows of vanished parents. There is nothing for it but to try and see through our missions to the end, as best we can, for until we do so, we will be permitted no calm.

So Christopher Banks, hero of *When we were Orphans*, summarises his life.[2]

The orphan spirit is a spirit of drivenness – the attempt to justify our existence and prove our acceptability through achievement and activity. This leads to unending drivenness – unending because no achievement or amount of activity can fully satisfy our need for acceptance. Usually this drivenness is developed in the households in which we grew up. From parents, children learn that certain behaviours are valued and others are not permitted. My dad's smile was certainly bigger when I came top of the class – second was not good enough! Let's examine five different types of drivenness:

THE PERFECTIONIST

In the household in which the Perfectionist grew up, the values were success, achievement, autonomy or 'being in control' and competition. Alongside this were the injunctions: 'Don't play' (it's the winning that counts, not the taking part!); 'Don't be spontaneous'; 'Don't fail or make mistakes'; and 'Don't rely on others' (they might let you down and cause you to fail). The child believes that unless they behave in the approved way then love and acceptance will be withdrawn, and certain fears develop.

Their fears:

- Loss of control
- Not being told what's going on
- Failure to achieve goals

• Things not being done right.

A good friend of mine has some of this in her background, as do I. She was cooking a meal for several of us and I asked if I could help. She said I could wash and cut up the strawberries. A straightforward enough task, you might think, but I know my friend and so I asked if there was any particular way she wanted the strawberries washed and cut up! Having received her 'No' to this question I proceeded to remove the stems, cut the strawberries in half and put them in the colander for washing. 'You've cut them before you washed them!' my friend exclaimed. 'That's the way I do it,' I replied. 'But they will lose vitamin C.' 'They can take a pill!' I rejoined.

My friend said no more but secretly she was wishing she hadn't accepted my offer of help and done it herself. Perfectionists often end up doing everything themselves because they do not trust others to do tasks to their standards. One woman on a stress management course said that the day had been helpful but disturbing. She had thought, before the course, that her stress was caused by other people (especially her husband) leaving her to do everything herself. Having identified herself as a perfectionist she now realised that whenever he had tried to help she had criticised him for not doing it right and now he didn't even bother to offer!

Under pressure, Perfectionists can become arrogant, sarcastic and any ability to multi-task disappears as they become more single-minded and rigid.

THE PEOPLE PLEASER

The values of the People Pleaser are co-operation, consideration, and the serving of others. Alongside these are the injunctions: 'Don't be awkward – fit in'; 'Don't say no'; 'Avoid conflict'; and 'Don't be *you*, be who we need you to be'.

Their fears:

- Rejection or criticism
- Not being liked or included
- Being thought 'awkward'
- Conflict
- Upsetting people

People Pleasers are very easy to be with or have in a team but are often pulled this way and that by the different people they are trying to please, finding it very difficult to say 'No'. They are reluctant to challenge wrong ideas and try to anticipate what will please others, without checking first.

Under pressure, People Pleasers are likely to become more emotional and go into 'rescuing' behaviour.

THE ACTIVIST

The values of the Activist are energy, speed, activity and efficiency. They are always on the go and their idea of relaxation is to go for a run or workout at the gym. Alongside these values are the injunctions: 'Don't stop or be still'; 'Don't waste time'; 'Don't think or plan'; and 'Take short cuts'.

Their fears:

- Having nothing to do
- Wasting time
- Time to think
- Boredom

I can often pick out the Activists at the start of a course because they are late! They don't intend being late, but have a dread of being early as that would be a waste of precious time. As a result they plan to arrive exactly on time, but they consistently underestimate how long it will take them to get anywhere and how much time particular tasks will take. Activist drivers are unlikely to have planned their journey, expecting to work things out as they go along, will tend to drive in the fast lane and above the speed limit and will go ten miles out of their way to avoid sitting in stationary traffic!

Under pressure, Activists become more frenetic, with much visible activity but little achieved.

THE SAVIOUR

The values of a 'Saviour' are strength, courage, reliability and independence. A saviour is often self-sufficient; solitary; reliable; helpful whilst unable to accept help and able to problem-solve around difficult personal issues and make 'unpleasant' decisions. They hate admitting any weakness and get overloaded rather than ask for help. The dying words of a Saviour are 'I'm fine!' Alongside these values are the injunctions: 'Don't be weak or vulnerable'; 'Don't show emotion'; 'Don't let others down'; and 'Don't ask for help'.

Their fears:

- Their own vulnerability or weakness
- Not coping
- Letting people down
- Asking for help

This is the area in which God has had to challenge me the most. I remember one occasion when I had booked myself to go on a 'Women in Mission' conference on the three days immediately after a hospital operation. It didn't occur to me that I wouldn't cope. During a phone call to a friend prior to the operation, she asked how I was going to get to the conference. My declaration that I intended to drive brought a resounding 'Don't be an idiot, you are not allowed to drive within 24 hours of a general anaesthetic – you'll have to ask someone for a lift.' The thought of asking a total stranger for a lift and expecting them to come out of their way to pick me up was horrific to me, and yet my friend persuaded me that no other course of action was open to me. Learning to receive help has been a difficult but joyful journey.

Under pressure, Saviours withdraw and stop communicating. They don't want help, because if you were close enough to help you'd also be close enough to see the mess. They prefer to sort themselves out in solitude and only reappear when they have got themselves together.

THE STRIVER

The values of a 'Striver' are determination, endurance, and effort. I suspect that whenever, in childhood, they pushed a parental boundary, it moved. Usually they are intense – committed to righting wrongs. They love any new or different task but their initial interest wears off before they finish. In their communication with others they are likely to go off at a tangent and forget their original objective. Alongside their values are the injunctions: 'Don't give up or give in'; 'Don't succeed or fail' (the job is never over and so cannot be evaluated); and 'Don't relax'.

Their fears:

- Not having put in enough effort
- Being thought irresponsible
- Giving up
- Finishing

Under pressure, they put in more and more effort, but often change course before anything is achieved.

MAKING COFFEE

A caricature of each different self-expectation can be seen in the way they go about getting coffee for a small group of eight people:

The Perfectionist: Out comes the notepad to record each person's order. A request for 'a milky coffee' requires more specific information 'Is that half an inch of milk or a full inch?' Whilst waiting for the kettle to boil they will arrange the mugs in the order in which people are sitting and may even turn all the handles to face the same direction because that's neat – isn't it?

The People Pleaser is already in the kitchen making coffee for the group. No one suggested coffee, they just anticipated the group's wants and got on with it. They appear with a tray of coffees and a big smile. Do not refuse their coffee! It will elicit disappointment and a sad 'But I've made you one'.

The Activist dashes to the kitchen calling out 'I'll make coffee' over their shoulder. In the kitchen they realise they're not exactly clear what each person wanted so rather than check they decide to make a few of each. In their rush they forgot the tray but are not going to waste time going to get one when a balancing act of four mugs down each arm would be much quicker. If they make it through the two sets of doors you'll get 'whatever' very quickly, but there is the chance they will drop the lot!

The Saviour failed to realise that they were thirsty and when someone else offers to make them coffee says 'No, I'm fine; I'll make myself one in a minute – thanks.'

Never send a *Striver* for coffee! They go to the kitchen, switch on the kettle and open the cupboard containing the mugs. 'It's about time this cupboard was given a good clean out' they decide. In cleaning out the cupboard they come across Fred's mug. Now Fred moved away a week or so ago, but was very fond of his mug. They decide to send it to him and search for his address and wrapping material ... The kettle boiled two months ago, but coffee never got made!

THE PROBLEM

Over time our self-expectation has become our way of feeling good about ourselves. It is our learned strategy for earning acceptance, approval and love from others and from God. Whilst there is nothing wrong with having the ability to do things to a high standard, with pleasing others, with having the ability to do a lot of things very quickly, with having the capacity to take on responsibility and with the desire to put in a lot of effort, when these things become our way of making life work they are sinful. God has provided *the* way in which we become acceptable to Him through the cross of Christ. Any self-reliant strategy is unacceptable to Him and needs to be repented of.

CASE STUDY: PAUL

> We do not want you to be uninformed, brothers, about the hardships we suffered in the province of Asia. We were under great pressure, far beyond our ability to endure, so that we despaired even of life. Indeed, in our hearts we felt the sentence of death. *But this happened that we might not rely on ourselves but on God, who raises the dead.* He has delivered us from such a deadly peril, and he will deliver us. On him we have set our hope that he will continue to deliver us, as you help us by your prayers. Then many will give thanks on our behalf for the gracious favour granted us in answer to the prayers of many. (2 Cor. 1:8–11, my italics)

PERSONAL APPLICATION

I believe that God often allows pressure in our lives for just such a purpose as Paul discovered: to cause us to drop our self-reliant strategies and to rely on God alone. How do we do this? Firstly, we have to destroy the power of these strategies through repentance and secondly, we have to learn a new pattern of God-reliance.

REPENTANCE

You may find the following prayer helpful:

Lord, thank You that You have gifted me with the ability to do things to a high standard/with pleasing others/with having the ability to do a lot of things very quickly/with having the capacity to take on responsibility/with the desire to put in a lot of effort. I realise I have allowed these capacities to become my way of making life work and feeling good about myself. I'm sorry that I chose to rely on myself and not on You. Please forgive me and help me to work out a new pattern of thinking and behaving that knows and declares that Christ's death on the cross is my only means of becoming acceptable and the only strategy for making life work. Amen.

NEW PATTERNS

- Ask God to show you when you are falling back into self-reliance.
- Find an accountability group and ask for their support.
- Begin to confront some of the fears in prayer – especially the fear of rejection.
- Begin to confront some of the fears in action – delegate, ask for help, stop, say 'No', take time to relax.
- Plant God's Word in place of the old messages.

ADOPTED AS SONS

For you did not receive a spirit that makes you a slave again to fear, but you received the Spirit of sonship. And by him we cry, 'Abba, Father.' The Spirit himself testifies with our spirit that we are God's children. (Rom. 8:15–16)

The knowledge that we are adopted as God's children through Christ's death and resurrection frees us from having to earn our acceptance through achievement and activity. We start from a place of acceptance, belonging and security! As we sustain our relationship with God through worship, prayer, Bible reading and fellowship, we become secure in the knowledge of God's love for us – our true identity. As we remain in that love and obey Christ's commands we cannot help but be fruitful, for 'This is to my Father's glory, that you bear much fruit, showing yourselves to be my disciples' (John 15:8). Yet this good fruit is the result of abiding, not striving.

CHAPTER 6

LACK OF PURPOSE/ DEMOTIVATION AND RESENTMENT

LACK OF PURPOSE/DEMOTIVATION

Have you ever wondered 'What's the point?' You clean the house and it soon gets messed up again; you write a report that no one bothers to read; you put in a new business proposal knowing that your manager is not open to change; you preach a sermon to which no one listens; or you discipline your children wondering if their behaviour will ever change. It is a question that has perplexed scholars and philosophers down the ages. It is a question reflected in films such as *Groundhog Day* – is each day doomed to be a repeat of the last, with few consequences and no purpose? The writer of Ecclesiastes, generally thought to be Solomon (the wisest man of his time) set himself the goal of studying and personally experiencing everything that could possibly give his life meaning – pleasure, work, achievement, riches etc. and came to the following conclusion: "'Meaningless! Meaningless!" says the Teacher. "Utterly meaningless! Everything is meaningless'" (Eccl.1:2) or, as Billy Crystal put it in the film *City Slickers*, 'Is this the best that it gets?'

Lack of purpose can be both a symptom of stress and a cause. When we see little point in what we are doing then we bring no energy to it and it weighs heavy on our spring. According to Dr Herbert Freudenburg, to be engaged each day in activities that seem meaningless is an almost certain prescription for burnout.[1] When we lack purpose we feel a void in our lives and try to fill the emptiness with anything that can offer temporary comfort – such as food, alcohol, possessions ...

FAVOUR

God answers the futility of our lives with His favour. The psalmist asks that God 'satisfy us in the morning with [His] unfailing love' (Psa. 90:14) and 'May the favour of the Lord our God rest upon us; establish the work of our hands for us – yes, establish the work of our hands' (Psa. 90:17). God can permeate everything we do, say and are, with meaning and purpose – a purpose that will last beyond death if we are willing to allow Him to direct us. The story of the captive servant girl in 2 Kings 5 illustrates how God can use each of our lives. She has been captured, taken away from home and family and made to work for Naaman's wife as a servant. If she had had hopes and plans for her life they had come to nothing. Yet it is here in this captive situation that God established the work of her hands. She obviously serves her master and mistress well and cares for them – enough to risk speaking out and suggesting that he seek a cure for his leprosy from Elisha, God's prophet. God gave her life purpose and her story has encouraged and challenged millions down the centuries.

A few years ago I had the opportunity to co-lead a session on 'Does my work matter to God?' at Spring Harvest at Work Together. One man came up after the session and spoke of how he had arrived at the conference depressed and ready to give up on his job. Yet his sense of purpose and motivation had been renewed as we studied the value of our work in the session and now he knew that he was doing the work to which he was called. Let's remind ourselves of the value God places on our work:

- Provision for ourselves (2 Thess. 3:7–10), our families (1 Tim. 5:8) and others (Deut. 14:28–29)
- Stewardship of people and of our planet (Gen. 2:15)
- Enjoyment (Eccl. 3:22)
- Opportunity to do good (Gal. 6:10)
- Participating in God's work (Eph. 2:10)
- Service (Eph. 4:12)
- An agent of change in society – subversive (salt)

God can also redirect our paths. Eighteen years ago I was studying Isaiah when the verse 'Why spend money on what is not bread, and your labour on what does not satisfy?' (Isa. 55:2) seemed to leap off the page. I felt that God was telling me to change jobs, but was resistant to the upheaval involved. The next day when I got into work I was made redundant! I was given one month's money and told to clear my desk. It was a scary time yet I knew that God had forewarned me. There followed a month of listening to God to understand the next step and paying attention to all that He was showing me through circumstances and Bible reading. Now

I am able to spend my labour on work that satisfies, though all work has elements that seem unnecessary or uninteresting!

The writer of Ecclesiastes may have concluded that 'under the sun' everything is meaningless, yet, in the light of eternity, it is God who can establish the work of our hands and give our life meaning.

RESENTMENT

Resentment can creep in in numerous ways – someone is not pulling their weight in the team; I'm given a particularly difficult/ boring/unpleasant task and no one else is; I'm 'expected' to put other people's dirty washing in the basket when they just leave it on the bedroom floor; I can't afford to go out for a meal with friends; I've been unjustly accused; I'm tired and they should have realised; it's just not fair … The list goes on. Talking with delegates on stress courses I have begun to realise the extent of this stressor. Comments like 'We've gone through massive changes in our department and it's not change I mind – it's that this change is making things worse not better and I resent all the work involved'; or 'Because I am reliable, my manager always asks me to do things and other members of the team are free- loading'; or 'I'm part-time so all my friends think I'm available to take in deliveries/mind grandchildren/give lifts …'.

Resentment soon leads to bitterness. As we rehearse the wrongs and perceived-wrongs done to us we dig a well of bitterness. The doctors of the Minirth–Meier clinic call bitterness, which is the result of holding grudges, 'the most significant factor in burnout'.[2] How then are we to rid ourselves of resentment and bitterness? God's answer is forgiveness.

FORGIVENESS

Catherine Marshall in her book *Something More*[3] was the first to help me understand the importance of forgiveness. Firstly, I saw that to forgive was not an optional extra in the Christian life – in fact our own forgiveness depends on it as the parable of the unmerciful servant (Matt. 18:21–35) and the Lord's Prayer illustrate. But more than understanding, she gave me a practical 'how to' lesson. Forgiveness does not depend on our feelings – it is a legal transaction. I hand over my right to be judge and jury on another person's behaviour, to God. It is helpful to list what that 'behaviour' is so I write the person's name at the top of a page and then note down all the things (acts of omission and commission) as well as the consequences of those actions (whether intended or not) together with any hurt I have experienced. I spend time waiting on the Lord to see if there is anything else that should be on the list and then I burn the list to symbolise handing over judgment to God. A prayer along the lines of

> Father God, I choose to release X from my judgment. Forgive me for any way in which my lack of forgiveness has hampered Your work in my life or theirs. I now ask You to bless them. Amen.

seals the transaction. When the devil tries to remind me of items on the list, I remind him that the list is now burned and God has taken over the case!

Unforgiveness is like an emotional black hole. Emotional energy is still being poured into situations, relationships, disagreements, and so on that physically ended years ago leaving people emotionally handicapped as they face the present and the future. Ephesians 4:31–32 is not just a suggestion – it is vital for emotional and spiritual health:

> Get rid of all bitterness, rage and anger, brawling and slander, along with every form of malice. Be kind and compassionate to one another, forgiving each other, just as in Christ God forgave you.

CASE STUDY: JOSEPH

If anyone had reason to feel demotivated and resentful it must have been Joseph: he is attacked and sold into slavery by his brothers; taken to a foreign country; wrongfully accused of rape; his reputation is in shreds when Potiphar believes his wife's lies about Joseph; he is imprisoned and forgotten, and his dreams are dashed. No one would blame him for wondering if his life really has any point. He was wronged at every stage and did nothing to deserve this as he explains to his fellow prisoner, the cupbearer:

> Within three days Pharaoh will lift up your head and restore you to your position, and you will put Pharaoh's cup in his hand, just as you used to do when you were his cupbearer. But when all goes well with you, remember me and show me kindness; mention me to Pharaoh and get me out of this prison. For I was forcibly carried off from the land of the Hebrews, and even here I have done nothing to deserve being put in a dungeon. (Gen. 40:13–15)

Joseph's reaction to the injustice of his situation is instructive. Firstly, even though he had no choice about the work he did, he worked for both Potiphar and for the prison warder as if working for the Lord. He gained their favour and they made him responsible for everything within their household or prison

– leadership training that prepared him for when he was put in charge of all Egypt! He shunned sin, ie sleeping with Potiphar's wife. It could have been so easy to think that all the hardships in his life merited a little pleasure when it was offered. He forgave his brothers and wanted good for them, making provision for them in time of famine. And through it all he learned to trust himself to God's timing and God's plan. 'And now, do not be distressed and do not be angry with yourselves for selling me here, because it was to save lives that God sent me ahead of you ... So then, it was not you who sent me here, but God.' (Gen. 45:5,8)

PERSONAL APPLICATION

- Take time to allow God to restore your sense of purpose and motivation by asking Him to show you the value He places on the different roles you have.
- If there is any part of your work that seems pointless, ask your manager or someone with a broader overview to help you find the purpose in it. It may even be that the purpose is now obsolete and the task can be discontinued.
- Remember that we work 'as for the Lord' and God is more concerned with 'how' we do our work than 'what' we do.
- Learn to recognise resentment and bitterness before they have a chance to fester. Turn any desire to curse into a prayer of blessing.
- Keep short accounts – forgive others as God has forgiven you.
- Allow God to cleanse you from all bitterness and pour His healing into any wounds.
- Know that while others plot our downfall, God is able to use

everything for good: 'You intended to harm me, but God intended it for good to accomplish what is now being done, the saving of many lives.' (Gen. 50:20)

CHAPTER 7

PHYSICAL AND SPIRITUAL ATTACK

As Christians we are engaged in a spiritual battle:

> 'I [Jesus] have given them your word and the world has hated them, for they are not of the world any more than I am of the world. My prayer is not that you take them out of the world but that you protect them from the evil one.' (John 17:14–15)

Alan Redpath also alerts us to this fact:

> Every Christian is exposed to the attack of the enemy of souls in his service for the Lord. I remember years ago I prayed, 'Lord, never take me to any sphere of Christian work for Thee in which Satan is not interested, because if he isn't interested, then I surely could never be in Thy will.' Believe me, that prayer has been answered a hundredfold, much more than I bargained for! [1]

The greatest danger is not to realise that we are at war. America was most vulnerable to attack when it thought that it was not yet in the Second World War and Japan took full advantage of this at Pearl Harbor. As Christians we are most vulnerable to attack when we have succumbed to false teaching that implies that health, wealth and prosperity are our right and that the Christian life is a bed of roses!

THE DEVIL'S STRATEGY

In order to fight we need to study the devil's strategies. They are threefold:

- Direct attack on our relationship with God
- Attack via our own sinful nature
- Attack through others

1) DIRECT ATTACK

This spiritual battle goes right back to the Garden of Eden and it is there we have to start if we are to understand this direct attack on our relationship with God:

> Now the serpent was more crafty than any of the wild animals the LORD God had made. He said to the woman, 'Did God really say, "You must not eat from any tree in the garden"?' The woman said to the serpent, 'We may eat fruit from the trees in the garden, but God did say, "You must not eat fruit from the tree that is in the middle of the garden, and you must not touch it, or you will die."' 'You will not surely die,' the serpent said to the woman. 'For God knows that when you eat of it your eyes will be opened, and you will be like God, knowing good and evil.' (Gen. 3:1–5)

His first line of attack is to throw doubt on God's Word. He misquotes God: 'You must not eat from *any* tree … ' and then he denies what God has said: 'Did God really say …' Doubting God's Word is like stepping off a rock into quicksand – we have no firm foundation. We are told that 'All Scripture is God-breathed and is useful for teaching, rebuking, correcting and training in righteousness, so that the man of God may be thoroughly equipped for every good work' (2 Tim. 3:16). Sometimes our doubt of God's Word is shown, not in questioning what is written, but in not bothering to read it. We doubt its relevance to our lives and question the usefulness of time spent studying it. Without God's Word planted deeply in our minds and spirits we are ill-equipped to counter the devil.

His second line of attack is to question God's character. 'For God knows that when you eat of it your eyes will be opened.' In effect the devil is saying 'God is withholding something good from you – if He were really good He would have allowed you this fruit.' All sin starts with the suspicion that God is not good and leads on to our 'supplementing' God's 'inadequate' provision through our own action – we take what we believe a truly loving God should have provided for us anyway!

Having undermined God's Word and His character, the devil now offers us self-sufficiency and knowledge: '… you will be like God, knowing good and evil.' Deep down there is something in us that hates being God-dependent – we want to be our own god and be in charge of our own destiny. Sadly we fail to realise that sin does not lead to control of our destiny – we have just handed over our life for enemy occupation.

2) OUR SINFUL NATURE

Once Adam and Eve have disobeyed God and eaten of the fruit, the sinful nature kicks in in two ways: hiding from God and avoiding responsibility for their actions. Why did they hide? 'I heard you in the garden, and I was afraid because I was naked; so I hid' (Gen. 3:10). Interestingly, Adam was not physically naked at this point because he and Eve had made garments for themselves from fig leaves, yet they knew that they were spiritually naked and without protection from God's omniscient gaze. When they realise that there is no hiding from God, they attempt to avoid all responsibility for their actions – Adam blames Eve and God ('The woman you put here with me') and Eve blames the serpent. If you have ever listened to yourself justify your sin you may, like me, be amazed at your own creativity! I can find myriad reasons why sin is not my fault, or why it is too minor a thing for God to be concerned with. I become like the man caught speeding who complained to the police: 'Wouldn't your time be better spent catching real criminals!' More often though, I just hide – I cut the lines of communication between myself and God. God, however, has many and varied ways of getting our attention, as Balaam (through a talking donkey), Jonah (inside a great fish) and Peter (when a cock crowed) found out.

3) ATTACK THROUGH OTHERS

Already we can see the seeds of relationship break down as Adam and Eve try to avoid blame. This continues through Genesis as Cain's anger leads him to murder his brother. Throughout the Old Testament the people of God face attack from other nations and civil war between the twelve tribes. The only times they know peace are when they are living in obedience to God's law and within the loving provision of His covenant. By the time we reach the chronological end of the Old Testament, with the book of Nehemiah in 446 BC: 'Those who survived the exile and are back in the province are in great trouble and disgrace. The wall of Jerusalem is broken down, and its gates have been burned with fire' (Neh. 1:3). This description may reflect the lives of many individual Christians today as well as parts of God's Church. At this stage the devil no longer needs to attack – we pose no threat to him.

What walls are broken down in our own lives and the life of the Church? Is it the wall of obedience and personal holiness; the wall of prayer; the wall of distinctiveness from the world; the wall of unity or Christian fellowship; or the wall of faith? When the walls are broken down our defences are gone and the devil is free to walk in and take whatever he wants – our health, our relationships, our work or our homes. Our sinfulness has given him the right of entry.

GOD'S PROTECTION

If these are the devil's strategies, how are we to mount a defence? We cannot! In our own strength we cannot resist the devil, but when we recognise that the battle belongs to the Lord, we can follow the instructions of our heavenly commander, as Nehemiah did.

1) Nehemiah faced the reality of the situation – the walls broken down, the gates burned and the people in disgrace. Sometimes we fail to realise quite how far we have drifted away from God and allowed our lives to become compromised. We may need a messenger, as Nehemiah had, or a wake-up call to alert us to the true state of affairs. It may even be that stress is God's wake-up call.

2) Nehemiah mourned and fasted and prayed, confessing his and the people's sin:

> 'I confess the sins we Israelites, including myself and my father's house, have committed against you. We have acted very wickedly towards you. We have not obeyed the commands, decrees and laws you gave your servant Moses.' (Neh. 1:6–7)

Nehemiah knows that the enemy only had opportunity to take ground because of disobedience and rebellion. Just as the devil's strategy starts with undermining our relationship with God, so ours needs to start by putting it right. We do so at the cross of Christ in humility and repentance. Note that repentance and remorse are different. Remorse regrets that we didn't get away with it and are suffering the consequences – repentance acknowledges that we were wrong to do it and have broken God's law.

3) He waited for God's timing. It was four months between Nehemiah praying and the opportunity to present his request to the king. Often, when we have spent months or years going our own way, we expect God to 'jump to it' and put everything right when we repent and pray!

4) He put faith before fear. Being sad before the king was punishable by death and so when the king notices that Nehemiah looks sad he is understandably afraid and yet declares the truth:

> I was very much afraid, but I said to the king, 'May the king live for ever! Why should my face not look sad when the city where my fathers are buried lies in ruins, and its gates have been destroyed by fire?' (Neh. 2:3)

It isn't always easy to put faith before fear, but I believe that it was Nehemiah's time of waiting and praying that gave him the courage to do this. I was speaking to a Romanian pastor whose life had been threatened by the secret police because of his clear preaching of the gospel – a very real threat as he knew, having just conducted the funeral of a fellow pastor for whom an 'accident' had been arranged. Though inwardly fearful, his reply to the police was: 'You cannot threaten me with heaven!' Courage comes from knowing that our ultimate destiny is secure in God's hands.

5) '"Let us start rebuilding." So they began this good work' (Neh. 2:18). Rebuilding the broken walls around our lives takes work – the hard ongoing labour of putting each brick in place. The names of some of those who built the wall are instructive: Jedaiah meaning 'invoker of God', a man of prayer; Benjamin meaning 'son of my right hand' – one who is there to protect; and Zadok meaning 'justice' or integrity. It takes commitment to a 'disciple' lifestyle of studying and obeying God's Word, communicating with Him in prayer, and living with integrity, if we are to rebuild the walls of God's protection. If all of this sounds onerous, then perhaps we have already allowed the devil to distort our view of our loving heavenly Father and replace it with that of an overbearing taskmaster. The work I am speaking of is no different from the work that a couple will put into a good marriage to ensure its security and health – work that is not a duty but a joy!

6) Removing the rubble (Neh. 4:10). In order to rebuild on a firm foundation we have to remove the rubble that has accumulated in our lives. Only the Lord can show us what is rubble and what is a valuable building block that is in the wrong place. The rubble includes wrong relationships, habitual sins, addictive behaviours,

wrong attitudes to God, pride and idols.

It is as we start rebuilding that the devil resumes his attack because there is no battle until the Christian engages in God's work, seeks His glory and is concerned for His people. Firstly, there's ridicule and insults (Neh. 4:1–3); then, disillusionment and tiredness (Neh. 4:10); thirdly, plotting and covert attacks (Neh. 4:11); and finally, fear (Neh. 4:12). The experience of many Christians that I have spoken to is that it is as they are about to engage in some God-ordained work that the attack comes – the argument with a family member, the letter of criticism from a member of the congregation, the sudden illness, etc. During a university mission week, I was grateful to the student who alerted me one evening to the devil's use of illness in preventing a fellow student coming to the Christian gospel presentations. The very next morning another student, whom I had been due to meet, cancelled due to illness. I decided to go to her house to see her, despite her cold, and had the privilege of leading her to Christ.

7) Prayer cover and encouragement. Nehemiah does not try to fight the enemy single-handed. He organises God's people for their own protection, designating some to work while others kept watch with their weapons at the ready:

Therefore I stationed some of the people behind the lowest points of the wall at the exposed places, posting them by families, with their swords, spears and bows. After I looked things over, I stood up and said to the nobles, the officials and the rest of the people, 'Don't be afraid of them. Remember the Lord, who is great and awesome, and fight for your brothers, your sons and your daughters, your wives and your homes.' When our enemies heard that we were aware of their plot and that God had frustrated it, we all returned to the wall, each to his own work. From that day on, half of my men did the work, while the other half were equipped with spears, shields, bows and armour. The officers posted themselves behind all the people of Judah who were building the wall. Those who carried materials did their work with one hand and held a weapon in the other, and each of the builders wore his sword at his side as he worked. But the man who sounded the trumpet stayed with me. (Neh. 4:13–18)

In response to ridicule and insults, they prayed (Neh. 4:4–5,9). To fend off disillusionment and tiredness, they kept watch (Neh. 4:9). To face plots and covert attacks, they armed themselves (Neh. 4:13, 16, 18, 21). The weapons of faith, the gospel, salvation and truth are powerful indeed (Eph. 6:10–20). In response to fear, they exercised faith: 'Our God will fight for us!' (Neh. 4:20).

We are all engaged in an intense spiritual warfare in which there will be no armistice until we reach heaven. Satan hurls all his fiery darts at the child of God who is abandoned to the will of God, and at the church which is concerned to have a soul-winning ministry. This will mean that in the course of the battle there will be grave wounds, much suffering and hurt, many things that grieve us and break our heart, but nothing matters except that we should stand our ground and remain victorious on the field. What a day it will be when the Lord welcomes us home![2]

PERSONAL APPLICATION

- Do a survey of the walls around your life – are they in good repair or are the gates burned and the walls breached?

- Come before God in mourning, prayer and repentance if personal or corporate sin has caused the walls to be in ruins.

- Be careful not to allow the enemy to undermine your belief in God's character or His Word.

- Ensure that it is God's work we are carrying out and not some pet initiative of our own – perhaps seeking out wise mentors who can help bring wisdom on this.

- The attack may take a variety of forms: ridicule, insults, disillusionment, tiredness, covert plotting, threats or direct assault.

- Expect spiritual attack when carrying out God's work (it goes with the territory!) yet God's protection is real and powerful.

- God has provided armour for us: 'Finally, be strong in the Lord and in his mighty power. Put on the full armour of God so that you can take your stand against the devil's schemes. For our struggle is not against flesh and blood, but against the rulers, against the authorities, against the powers of this dark world and against the spiritual forces of evil in the heavenly realms' (Eph. 6:10–12).

- Remember that our God is 'great and awesome' (Neh. 4:14).

- Watch and pray.

- Get prayer cover from others.

CHAPTER 8

STRENGTHENING THE SPRING

Whilst it is essential to examine each of the weights on the spring and to reduce the pressure they exert we should not ignore the spring itself. Strengthening the spring enables us to carry the load more effectively and without strain. The spring can be strengthened in numerous ways: physically, emotionally, intellectually and spiritually.

PHYSICALLY

It is not good to be preoccupied with our bodies, and yet some of us take too little care of this temple of the Holy Spirit. Our bodies are entrusted to us – they are the place we will live for the rest of our lives. Good stewardship of this gift from God requires us to care for our bodies and our health. The principles for this are well known: healthy diet, drink plenty of water, exercise, sufficient sleep;

fresh air and daylight. Rarely, for any of us, is the issue one of 'not knowing' how to look after ourselves. No, it's that we fail to give it priority or lack the discipline to exercise regularly, eat healthily and get to bed on time. I know that personally this priority is most likely to reassert itself after a period of illness as I acknowledge that the cough/cold/chest infection could have been avoided if I had been more consistent in healthy care of my physical self. A few questions to help us review this area:

- Are you constantly tired or lacking in energy?
- Are you more than 14 lb under- or over-weight?
- Does your diet contain a sufficient supply of fresh fruit and vegetables? (Most of us are now advised to take a multi-vitamin supplement.)
- Do you drink a litre of water a day (as water, not coffee or tea)?
- Do you take aerobic exercise three to five times a week for at least 30 minutes?
- Are you getting eight hours sleep a night?
- Do you get outside for at least 30 minutes a day?

EMOTIONALLY

The heart, as a bodily organ, is central to life – when it stops beating, this life is over. Our emotional heart serves an equally important role: 'Above all else, guard your heart, for it is the wellspring of life' (Prov. 4:23).

But how can we guard our heart? Living in this world will mean that we face hurts, grief, disappointments and betrayal. Luke 6:45 tells us that the heart is like a storehouse: 'The good man brings good things out of the good stored up in his heart, and the evil man brings evil things out of the evil stored up in his heart. For out of the overflow of his heart his mouth speaks.' The key seems to be in what we choose to 'store'. Things happen to us in this life but we have the choice as to whether we store our emotional reaction to them and inwardly rehearse our disappointments, loss and hurt, or whether we reach out to the hem of Jesus' garment as the woman with internal bleeding did in Mark 5, and allow Him to heal us.

God wants our hearts to be filled with peace and contentment: 'Do not let your hearts be troubled. Trust in God; trust also in me' (John 14:1) and 'Let the peace of Christ rule in your hearts' (Col. 3:15). Paul says that this peace or contentment can be learned: 'I have learned the secret of being content in any and every situation ... ' (Phil. 4:12). How? Patrick Klingaman points the way:

> Although the practice of contentment is challenging in our culture, learning contentment is conceptually quite simple. Three keys to cultivating contentment are gratitude, acceptance, and service.'[1]

Gratitude: '... give thanks in all circumstances' (1 Thess. 5:18). God doesn't need our thanks but we need to say thank you. Thankfulness to God changes us in a variety of ways. It reminds us that we are dependent on God for everything, our life, health, the food we eat ... and so helps counter any temptation to pride. Thanking God for past blessings and current situations opens us up to receive what He is doing and gives us expectancy for the future. When the barren woman of Isaiah 54 (Zion) is commanded to sing, she is still barren – she is not to await pregnancy before opening her mouth. Praise changes the situation because through it we declare our belief that God is in control. Anything other than praise attributes more power to people or to circumstances than to God.

Acceptance: Sometimes we can expend emotional energy thinking 'This should never have happened' or 'Why me?' instead of accepting the situation and asking God how we should respond to it. As the serenity prayer puts it: 'O God, give us serenity to accept what cannot be changed, courage to change what should be changed, and wisdom to distinguish the one from the other.'[2]

Service: When we serve God and others, our attention is turned from an inward focus on our own situation and problems to an outward focus on the needs of others. Being able to make a difference to their situations can change how we see our own.

INTELLECTUALLY

We can also strengthen our spring through learning new skills and widening our thinking and reading. 'Books shape us, dynamically moulding our minds and souls. You are never the same person when you finish a book – even one that is read purely for escape or entertainment. A conviction may take root or deepen, the imagination may be sparked, a new perspective may dawn. A.W. Tozer has aptly stated that "the things you read will fashion you by slowly conditioning your mind".'[3] Hence the decisions we make about what we read are vital if we are to be transformed by the renewing of our minds (Rom. 12:2).

Reading is not the only way we can learn – going on courses or being coached by others is also important. For instance, how many of us could save precious minutes or even hours in the day by having a better grasp of our computer's software packages?

SPIRITUALLY

> In fact, though by this time you ought to be teachers, you need someone to teach you the elementary truths of God's word all over again. You need milk, not solid food! Anyone who lives on milk, being still an infant, is not acquainted with the teaching about righteousness. But solid food is for the mature, who by constant use have trained themselves to distinguish good from evil. (Heb. 5:12–14)

Strengthening our spring spiritually is about becoming mature as a Christian. Maturity is not gained through the number of years we have been a Christian, it is dependent on our spiritual diet during that time. One eighteen-year-old I know is mentoring Christian women twice her age with an amazing God-given wisdom – her diet: three hours of prayer and Bible study every morning from 5 till 8 am. I'm not there yet! But I do know that we cannot expect to mature spiritually on a hasty five-minute reading of some daily devotional notes or a 'thought for the day' snack. It has never been easier to get good teaching in written or auditory form and we have the Bible on tape or CD – time spent travelling can be time spent strengthening our spiritual spring.

> Through the word of God the Spirit of God comes in fullness on your life, and occupies your heart. Here is the secret of all power in leadership: to be possessed by the Son of God, to be strengthened by His indwelling power, and to be filled by His Spirit. And here is the only way: 'Do not let this Book of the Law depart from your mouth; meditate on it day and night, so that you may be careful to do everything written in it. Then you will be prosperous and successful.' (Joshua 1:8) There is no shortcut to holiness.[4]

Will we take seriously the challenge to strengthen our spring and by careful stewardship, grow our physical, emotional, intellectual and spiritual health and strength?

CHAPTER 9

THE SUPPORT OF OTHERS

On one 'Insight into Stress' day at CWR I well remember the interaction of two delegates. One expressed the pressure she was feeling at having moved house and finding herself with a neighbour who seemed very interested in everything about her – this neighbour commented on the choice of curtains and other changes they were making to the house; she 'appeared' in the garden every time the delegate went into her garden and started up a conversation over the fence. The delegate felt that her privacy had been violated. 'Oh for such a neighbour!' was the heartfelt cry from another delegate. This woman, used to the community culture of an Arab country, now found herself in a well-to-do London suburb with a husband who was often away on business. 'I could die,' she said, 'and no one would know for days.'

So here is the paradox: as humans we are caught between the competing drives, the drive to belong, to fit in and be a part of something bigger than ourselves, and the drive to let our deepest selves rise up, to walk alone, to refuse the accepted and the comfortable, and this can mean for a time, the acceptance of anguish. It is in the group we discover what we have in common. It is as individuals that we discover a personal relationship with God. We must find a way to balance our two opposing impulses.[1]

Much of what we have examined so far, we have done so from the standpoint of the individual and so it is right that we now turn our attention to the role others play in supporting us in times of stress or excessive pressure. There is mutuality in this – the support I hope for and solicit from others is also the support I offer to others. When I ask people if they have a support network the most usual answer is a reference to their friends or immediate family. I think it can be helpful to focus on the support roles we may need as opposed to actual individuals. So what form might this support take?

Emotional: A shoulder to cry on; someone who is 'there for you'; a 'safe' person to tell how you feel; someone who believes in you. This usually will be a close friend or family member – someone who loves and accepts you as you are.

Logical: Someone to help you think through your situation; a wise counsellor; someone skilled in problem-solving techniques; a spiritual director or mentor. It can also include advice from a professional. This person may be a business colleague, a fellow professional, a trained counsellor or coach whose counsel is wise and objective. Many organisations now exist to support people with various illnesses or their families, giving valuable advice and sharing their experience.

Practical: This person takes some of the tasks off your hands or sees more effective ways of getting the job done. They provide a helping hand. I remember one time when my car, having got me to a training course, 'died' and I had to be towed back home by the RAC. Help! I was due to drive to another course the next day, then go from there to Gatwick, catch a flight to Germany for the holiday weekend, return late Monday and drive to a training venue on Tuesday. My neighbour, whom I did not know well, had seen my car being towed into the drive and enquired as to the problem. He then suggested that I did my travelling the next day by train while he towed my car to a local garage, had it fixed and paid for it on my behalf, and arranged for it to be back in my drive in good time for my return from Germany. Elijah's angel appeared to him in the desert – mine was alive and kicking in the flat next door!

Spiritual: They pray for you; remind you of your values and beliefs, and help you see the big picture. They challenge ungodly behaviour or attitudes and encourage you to seek God in the midst of the situation. Over the years I have become increasingly grateful for those who cover everything I am involved with in prayer, who challenge me when they feel I have taken on un-commanded work and who encourage me with their gentle enquiries as to how things have gone or how the book is coming along!

Friend: This is someone who cares about you; someone to laugh with, have fun with, and who takes you out of yourself. At a time of extreme pressure and bereavement in my life I remember one particular evening with a good friend – we were laughing so much at some situation that day that tears were rolling down our cheeks – when she lovingly said: 'Bev, it's so good to hear you laugh – I had begun to think that I would never hear it again.' She had helped me get back in touch with my laughter.

God never intended for us to live alone. Having declared everything else in His creation good, God then said, 'It is not good for … man to be alone.' We are designed to live within the context of family, community and church – we are part of Christ's Body.

> God has combined the members of the body and has given greater honour to the parts that lacked it, so that there should be no division in the body, but that its parts should have equal concern for each other. If one part suffers, every part suffers with it; if one part is honoured, every part rejoices with it. (1 Cor. 12:24–26)

The story is told of a man who was walking by the edge of some cliffs one day when he lost his footing and fell. Luckily he managed to grab hold of a small tree that was growing out of the cliff side. As he hung there, with the sea 100 feet below, he prayed that God might save him. Within minutes a man on the cliff above spotted him and offered to get a rope and lower it to him. 'No, it's all right, thank you – God is going to save me' was the reply, so the man continued his walk. A little while later a boat was passing underneath the man and the owner called out 'Jump into the sea and we will rescue you.' Again the man responded, 'No, it's all right, thank you – God is going to save me.' The boat went on its way and a little while later a helicopter saw the man and offered to let down its rope ladder. The reply was the same: 'No, it's all right, thank you – God is going to save me.' Eventually the man's arms grew tired and he lost his hold on the tree, fell into the sea below and drowned. Somewhat indignantly he approached the pearly gates and asked Peter why God had not saved him. Peter looked up his records and said, 'This is very strange, according to our records we sent you a man, a boat and a helicopter ...'

Are we open to receive the help God sends or does pride or fear of showing our vulnerability get in the way? In 2 Kings 5, Naaman, suffering from leprosy, went to Elisha to seek a cure. Elisha sent a messenger to tell him to wash seven times in the Jordan and his flesh would be restored. You would think that he would be delighted, but no! 'Namaan went away angry and said:

> 'I thought that he would surely come out to me and stand and call on the name of the LORD his God, wave his hand over the spot and cure me of my leprosy. Are not Abana and Pharpar, the rivers of Damascus, better than any of the waters of Israel? Couldn't I wash in them and be cleansed?' So he turned and went off in a rage.

Thankfully his servants persuaded him to wash in the Jordan and receive the healing that his pride and arrogance had nearly forfeited.

PERSONAL APPLICATION

- Spend time reflecting on your support network using the categories above.

- What type of support might you currently need?

- Ask God to show you where pride or fear of vulnerability is preventing you from receiving help.

- Sometimes we need to be proactive in seeking help rather than just waiting for the offer of assistance to come our way.

CHAPTER 10

FRUITFULNESS

You and I were designed to live fruitful lives: 'You did not choose me, but I [Jesus] chose you to go and bear fruit – fruit that will last' (John 15:16). The parable of the sower is well known to many of us, but let us revisit it as the parable of the ground. The seed is sown by God into the ground of our lives. The seed, we are told in Matthew 13:19 is the message of the kingdom – the truth of God's right to rule in our hearts and lives. What determines whether this seed will produce a crop of a 100, 60 or 30 times what was sown? The soil or ground.

The path: The ground is hard and the message about the kingdom is not understood, enabling the devil to snatch it away. The ground of our lives can become hard in a number of ways but often, at root, is rebellion against God and His authority:

'Today, if you hear his voice, do not harden your hearts as you did in the rebellion' (Heb. 3:15). Our very *self-expectation* can be the way we harden our hearts – determined to make our life work on our own terms, we rebel against God. Equally, *resentment* and bitterness can have a hardening effect.

Rocky places: The seed is received with joy but is unable to take root and so withers when trouble or persecution comes. The trouble that comes in this life may be in the form of *change* and loss, *demands and expectations* of others, or *spiritual attack*, but God can allow these things to highlight the shallowness of the soil and the abundance of rubble that has accumulated in our lives. Instead of praying for the trouble to be removed, switching our focus to the quality of the soil (*strengthening the spring*, especially spiritually) may prove to be the way forward.

Thorns: This represents 'those who hear, but as they go on their way they are choked by life's worries, riches and pleasures, and they do not mature' (Luke 8:14). Notice that pleasures are as great a danger as worries! Proverbs 24:30–31 gives us further understanding of this: 'I went past the field of the sluggard, past the vineyard of the man who lacks judgment; thorns had come up everywhere, the ground was covered with weeds, and the stone wall was in ruins.' Have the thorns entered our lives because of lack of watchfulness or judgment on our part, or laziness in allowing the walls of prayer and faith to fall down?

Good soil: Here lies the secret of fruitfulness – a crop of 100, 60 or 30 times what was sown. The question remains though, as to what we can do to ensure the quality of our soil.

The answer lies, I believe, in the way we respond to the pressures and hardships of this life. About eighteen years ago I went through the worst month of my life (though I now view it differently). Bereavement, loss of my house, financial crisis and redundancy followed each other in quick succession. Broken, I told God that I could have coped if they had come singly and questioned Him allowing them to come all at once. His reply: 'But this happened that we might not rely on ourselves but on God, who raises the dead' (2 Cor. 1:9). Gently, lovingly, as I learned to rely on Him (I wish I could claim credit for this but I had nowhere else to go!), I realised that He had allowed these events to break up the hard ground of my heart and fertilise the barren soil. I would not now be without that experience.

Recently I had the privilege of meeting an Irish woman who had 'lost' nine years of her life to ME. Part of that time was spent just sitting in a chair, her energy for the day having been completely exhausted in the effort to get up and move to the chair. Her story was one of gradual acceptance that God had allowed this, of forgiveness for friends who had abandoned her, 'forgot' to call or who just didn't understand, and of learning that all she had to give was the way she sat in her chair and the attitude with which she received help. I will never forget the way she looked in my eyes as she said, 'Bev, I thank God for those nine years and wouldn't be without them.' Before me sat a woman who had been through the fire and come out as gold, whose very presence was a blessing.

God chose us to bear fruit – fruit that is only possible as we learn to abide in Him. Pressures exist and the red warning light on our dashboard prompts us to open up the bonnet of our lives and check for the cause of the problem. Let me encourage you to allow stress to motivate you to seek God in new ways; to get away with Him and recover your life; to learn from Him how to live freely and lightly, enabling you to dance to the unforced rhythms of grace!

I would like to end this book with a quote, contained in a letter to his sister, from one of my spiritual heroes – Hudson Taylor, whose life was one of immense fruitfulness and whom God called to be a pioneer missionary in China.

The sweetest part ... is the rest which full identification with Christ brings. I am no longer anxious about anything, as I realise this; for He, I know, is able to carry out His will, and His will is mine. It makes no matter where He places me, or how. That is rather for Him to consider than for me; for in the easiest position He must give me His grace, and in the most difficult His grace is sufficient. It matters little to my servant whether I send him to buy a few cash worth of things, or the most expensive articles. In either case he looks to me for the money and brings me his purchases. So, if God should place me in serious perplexity, must He not give me much guidance; in positions of great difficulty, much grace; in circumstances of great pressure and trial, much strength? No fear that resources will prove unequal to the emergency! And His resources are mine, for He is mine, and is with me and dwells in me.[1]

NOTES

CHAPTER 1
1. *Tackling Work-related Stress* (HSE Books, 2006).
2. Stephen Williams and Lesley Cooper, *Managing Workplace Stress* (John Wiley and Sons Ltd, Chichester, 2002).
3. Harry Levinson, 'When Executives Burn Out', *Harvard Business Review* July–August 1996.
4. Christina Maslach, 'Burn-Out', *Human Behaviour*, Sept 1976, p.16.

CHAPTER 2
1. A.W. Pink, *Elijah* (The Banner of Truth Trust, Edinburgh, 1956) p.230.

CHAPTER 3
1. Elizabeth Kübler-Ross, *On Death and Dying* (Touchstone, London, 1997).
2. Jane Grayshon, *Treasures of Darkness* (Hodder & Stoughton, London, 1996) p.31.
3. *Indelible Ink* compiled by Scott Larsen (CWR, Surrey, 2005) p.27.

CHAPTER 4
1. Michael Lewis, 'It Boosts the Credibility', *Forbes ASAP*, Nov 30, 1998.
2. James Gleick, *Faster* (Little, Brown & Co, London, 1999).
3. David Kundtz, *Stopping* (Newleaf, Dublin, 1998).
4. Dallas Willard, *The Spirit of the Disciplines* (Hodder & Stoughton, London, 1996).
5. Jeannette Barwick and Beverley Shepherd, *Seasons of the Spirit* (CWR, Surrey, 2004).

CHAPTER 5
1. James Gleick, *Faster* (Little, Brown & Co, London, 1999).
2. Kazuo Ishiguro, *When we were Orphans* (Faber and Faber, London, 2000).

CHAPTER 6
1. Dr Herbert J. Freudenberger, *Burn-out: the high cost of high achievement* (Anchor/Doubleday, New York, 1980).
2. Frank Minirth, Paul Meier, Don Hawkins, Chris Thurman and Richard Flournoy, *Beating Burnout* (Inspirational Press, New York, 1997).
3. Catherine Marshall, *Something More* (Hodder & Stoughton, London, 1974).

CHAPTER 7
1. Alan Redpath, *Victorious Christian Service* (Pickering & Inglis, Glasgow, 1971) p.168.
2. Ibid., p.188.

CHAPTER 8
1. Patrick Klingaman, *Finding rest when the work is never done* (Victor Books, Colorado Springs, 2000).
2. Leith Anderson, *Making Happiness Happen* (Victor Books, Colorado Springs, 1987).
3. *Indelible Ink* compiled by Scott Larsen (CWR, Surrey, 2005) p.14.
4. Alan Redpath, *Victorious Christian Living* (Pickering & Inglis, Glasgow, 1956).

CHAPTER 9
1. Jean Vanier, *Becoming Human* (Darton, Longman and Todd, London, 1999).

CHAPTER 10
1. Dr and Mrs Howard Taylor, *Hudson Taylor's Spiritual Secret* (OMF Books, Discovery House Publishers, Grand Rapids, Michigan, 1990).

National Distributors

UK: (and countries not listed below)
CWR, Waverley Abbey House, Waverley Lane, Farnham, Surrey GU9 8EP. Tel: (01252) 784700
Outside UK (44) 1252 784700 Email: mail@cwr.org.uk

AUSTRALIA: KI Entertainment, Unit 21 317-321 Woodpark Road, Smithfield, New South Wales 2164.
Tel: 1 800 850 777 Fax: 02 9604 3699 Email: sales@kientertainment.com.au

CANADA: David C Cook Distribution Canada, PO Box 98, 55 Woodslee Avenue, Paris, Ontario N3L 3E5.
Tel: 1800 263 2664 Email: sandi.swanson@davidccook.ca

GHANA: Challenge Enterprises of Ghana, PO Box 5723, Accra. Tel: (021) 222437/223249
Fax: (021) 226227 Email: ceg@africaonline.com.gh

HONG KONG: Cross Communications Ltd, 1/F, 562A Nathan Road, Kowloon. Tel: 2780 1188
Fax: 2770 6229 Email: cross@crosshk.com

INDIA: Crystal Communications, 10-3-18/4/1, East Marredpalli, Secunderabad – 500026, Andhra
Pradesh. Tel/Fax: (040) 27737145 Email: crystal_edwj@rediffmail.com

KENYA: Keswick Books and Gifts Ltd, PO Box 10242-00400, Nairobi. Tel: (020) 2226047/312639
Email: sales.keswick@africaonline.co.ke

MALAYSIA: Canaanland, No. 25 Jalan PJU 1A/41B, NZX Commercial Centre, Ara Jaya, 47301
Petaling Jaya, Selangor. Tel: (03) 7885 0540/1/2 Fax: (03) 7885 0545 Email: info@canaanland.com.my

Salvation Publishing & Distribution Sdn Bhd, 23 Jalan SS 2/64, 47300 Petaling Jaya, Selangor.
Tel: (03) 78766411/78766797 Fax: (03) 78757066/78756360 Email: info@salvationbookcentre.com

NEW ZEALAND: KI Entertainment, Unit 21 317-321 Woodpark Road, Smithfield, New South Wales
2164, Australia. Tel: 0 800 850 777 Fax: +612 9604 3699 Email: sales@kientertainment.com.au

NIGERIA: FBFM, Helen Baugh House, 96 St Finbarr's College Road, Akoka, Lagos.
Tel: (01) 7747429/4700218/825775/827264 Email: fbfm_1@yahoo.com

PHILIPPINES: OMF Literature Inc, 776 Boni Avenue, Mandaluyong City. Tel: (02) 531 2183
Fax: (02) 531 1960 Email: gloadlaon@omflit.com

SINGAPORE: Alby Commercial Enterprises Pte Ltd, 95 Kallang Avenue #04-00, AIS Industrial Building,
339420. Tel: (65) 629 27238 Fax: (65) 629 27235 Email: marketing@alby.com.sg

SOUTH AFRICA: Struik Christian Books, 80 MacKenzie Street, PO Box 1144, Cape Town 8000.
Tel: (021) 462 4360 Fax: (021) 461 3612 Email: info@struikchristianmedia.co.za

SRI LANKA: Christombu Publications (Pvt) Ltd, Bartleet House, 65 Braybrooke Place, Colombo 2.
Tel: (9411) 2421073/2447665 Email: dhanad@bartleet.com

USA: David C Cook Distribution Canada, PO Box 98, 55 Woodslee Avenue, Paris, Ontario N3L 3E5,
Canada. Tel: 1800 263 2664 Email: sandi.swanson@davidccook.ca

CWR is a Registered Charity - Number 294387
CWR is a Limited Company registered in England - Registration Number 1990308

Courses and seminars

Publishing and new media

Conference facilities

Transforming lives

CWR's vision is to enable people to experience personal transformation through applying God's Word to their lives and relationships.

Our Bible-based training and resources help people around the world to:
• Grow in their walk with God
• Understand and apply Scripture to their lives
• Resource themselves and their church
• Develop pastoral care and counselling skills
• Train for leadership
• Strengthen relationships, marriage and family life and much more.

Our insightful writers provide daily Bible-reading notes and other resources for all ages, and our experienced course designers and presenters have gained an international reputation for excellence and effectiveness.

CWR's Training and Conference Centre in Surrey, England, provides excellent facilities in an idyllic setting – ideal for both learning and spiritual refreshment.

CWR Applying God's Word
to everyday life and relationships

CWR, Waverley Abbey House,
Waverley Lane, Farnham,
Surrey GU9 8EP, UK

Telephone: **+44 (0)1252 784700**
Email: **info@cwr.org.uk**
Website: **www.cwr.org.uk**

Registered Charity No 294387
Company Registration No 1990308

Waverley Abbey Insight Pamphlets

These handy pamphlets contain key practical insights on various issues taken from our *Waverley Abbey Insight Series* of books. Based on our proven counselling courses, these short guides will equip you to understand and address problems effectively. Packs of 10 – always keep them handy for helping sufferers or their friends/relatives.

A Brief Insight into Stress
ISBN: 978-1-85345-608-4

A Brief Insight into Depression
ISBN: 978-1-85345-609-1

A Brief Insight into Dementia
ISBN: 978-1-85345-610-7

A Brief Insight into Eating Disorders
ISBN: 978-1-85345-611-4

A Brief Insight into Addiction
ISBN: 978-1-85345-635-0

A Brief Insight into Anxiety
ISBN: 978-1-85345-641-1

A Brief Insight into Self-Esteem
ISBN: 978-1-85345-637-4

A Brief Insight into Bereavement
ISBN: 978-1-85345-639-8

8-panel pamphlets,
216x99mm, packs of 10

More in the *Waverley Abbey Insight Series*

Insight into Addiction
by Andre Radmall
ISBN: 978-1-85345-661-9

Insight into Anger
by Wendy Bray and Chris Ledger
ISBN: 978-1-85345-437-0

Insight into Anxiety
by Clare Blake and Chris Ledger
ISBN: 978-1-85345-662-6

Insight into Assertiveness
by Christine Orme and Chris Ledger
ISBN: 978-1-85345-539-1

Insight into Bereavement
by Wendy Bray and Diana Priest
ISBN: 978-1-85345-385-4

Insight Into Dementia
by Rosemary Hurtley
ISBN: 978-1-85345-561-2

Insight into Depression
by Chris Ledger and Wendy Bray
ISBN: 978-1-85345-538-4

Insight into Forgiveness
by Ron Kallmier and Sheila Jacobs
ISBN: 978-1-85345-491-2

Insight into Perfectionism
by Chris Ledger and Wendy Bray
ISBN: 978-1-85345-506-3

Insight into Self-esteem
by Chris Ledger and Wendy Bray
ISBN: 978-1-85345-663-3

**Insight into Helping Survivors
of Childhood Sexual Abuse**
by Wendy Bray and Heather Churchill
ISBN: 978-1-85345-692-3

Insight into Stress
by Beverley Shepherd
ISBN: 978-1-85345-790-6

For information on CWR's one-day Insight seminars visit www.cwr.org.uk/insightdays

For current prices visit www.cwr.org.uk/store
Available online or from a Christian bookshop

Help others with this handy reference guide

Benefit from Selwyn Hughes' many years of counselling and pastoral experience to help people with personal problems and to answer common objections when sharing your faith.

This handy guide will enable you to effectively address thirty-six frequently asked questions about:

- Depression
- Marriage
- Prayer
- Suffering and God's goodness
- Christ's divinity

and much more.

Includes numerous Scripture passages relevant to each topic. (Previously published as *The Pocket Guide for People Helpers*.)

What to Say When People Need Help
by Selwyn Hughes
98-page paperback,
197x129mm
ISBN: 978-1-85345-514-8

Your Personal Encourager
Selwyn Hughes

This classic bestseller will show you how to
encourage yourself and others in God. With more
than four decades of counselling experience,
Selwyn Hughes deals with 40 of life's most
common problems, including fear, disappointment
and bereavement, simply and effectively. Topics
include: When God seems far away, When hopes
are dashed, When doubts assail.

ISBN: 1-85345-072-3